God's Feminist Movement

Author

Daniel Hanson

Dan Hanson

available on

AMAZON.com

Published by Silver Palace Enterprises Worcester,

Massachusetts

TABLE OF CONTENTS

INTRODUCTION

GFM (God's Feminist Movement) is anti-feminist and is not meant to start a new women's movement. Using God's word, it teaches women how to achieve their utmost, rather than what they can get as the worldly feminist strive to do. This can be accomplished by beginning with the virtue God gave to all His daughters at their births and building upon that throughout their lives. The movements God intended His daughters to follow are revealed, so they are not ignorant of Satan's devices (II Corinthians 2:11). Nothing good came about when the serpent crept into the garden of Eden, and nothing good will ever come about when he creeps into God's churches. I chose this title because I have heard many women claim to be Christians and feminists. It is for them that I write to proclaim God's true design and worth for them to follow.

This book is intended to define the roles both men and women were created to fulfill, which, if accepted, can only lead to stronger marriages. Today, marriage is under severe attack, and many are being deceived, however, when we learn the truth, we are less likely to be caught in the web of deception. The chapters on Dating, Marriage, and Parenting were written to help you overcome the challenges often faced in these areas.

Each individual's relationship with God is personal. Don't have a personal relationship with God? Get one. Knowing His rules and following them can only lead us into a closer walk with Him.

Also provided are extraordinary reasons for young people to abstain from premarital sex. Giving them a higher regard for self is better than telling them not to have sex or threatening dire consequences if they do. They are the temples of God (I Corinthians 3:16) and God will destroy anyone who defiles His temple, including the owner (vs. 17). But God's mercy is infinite. If you did not abstain in the past and you can admit your mistakes then let God work in your life. You certainly have let Satan.

I have written this as a result of my observation of the effects of Satan's influence in the world but more importantly, within the church. From past experience, I know that with determination and genuine love things can be set right again. A gift of love is to make someone else's life better just as Jesus did. It is my determination that the church is following the world on the road to moral decay. My desire is to provide the guidance that is needed to whoever will listen. I write not because of the need but with the hope that I have something to offer that others do not. My approach is to provide a basis for wanting to fulfill God's designs for us as opposed to making someone do so out of the fear of failure. I am not pursuing humanism but firmly believe that walking in the ordinances of God can only result in a person being happier and healthier. I oppose anything that demotes man as loathsome such as Puritanism. It is my love for mankind and an overwhelming desire to show that love to the world that has inspired me to write.

It saddens my heart to see someone fall short of the glory God intended for her or him. Every little girl I see makes me desire to share with her what God has planned for her. I know she will face trials in her future. How can I keep from sharing God's wonderful Word with His little children? Other lovely values to share with a girl are found in the Proverbs 31 Woman. Such qualities will give her a new sense of her self-worth that will prove to be the ultimate inspiration for her to abstain from premarital sex. At the right time, in a young person's life, small things can make great changes, reaching into the rest of their lives. I heard a pastor on the radio say that if you are giving a teenager lickings, it is probably too late. Never put off until tomorrow what you can do today.

Hopefully, this book touches your life in a positive way and makes you rethink your value system. Too many ministers are not telling the whole truth as they should for fear of alienating people or losing their jobs. The church is not doing much better than the world. Presently, a girl who has been brought up as a member of a church is only 14% more likely to be a virgin on her wedding night than a nonreligious woman.[1] Only 8% of all brides are virgins on their wedding night. The good news is that even in this day and age, some women do save themselves for their husbands. Always tell your daughter that there is no reason she cannot do so as well. This is possible because Christ strengthens us so that we can do all things (Philippians. 4:13).

Have no doubt that something needs to be done to change these statistics; otherwise, nothing will ever change. Changing just one person will make it all worthwhile to me.

God's Feminist Movement is being presented as self-help guide despite not having any specific sequences of steps to follow. It's for your improvement and enlightenment. My ultimate goal is that parents will use it to guide their daughters. It's intended to be an interpretation of the way things should be and were meant to be. As you read, if you begin to question the ways of the world, then I have accomplished a lot. Some things in life we just

3

have to figure out on our own. I assume no responsibility for misinterpretation, misrepresentation or alteration.

Primarily, this book was designed to help those who are just becoming women and then, for those women who have lost their way. I have great hopes for the young and desire to show them God's truth. Having a guide helps them recognize when they are being led astray from the truth. It steers them away from making the same mistakes of those who went before them.

I did not write this book with the intention to be an affront to anyone; rather, it was written in true brotherly love. "The fear of the Lord is the beginning of knowledge: but fools despise wisdom and instruction" (Proverbs 1:7). Those growing into womanhood must be given guidance, regardless. I am aware that some women have difficulty accepting instructions from men on how to be godly women. This is not a book of charms; God has kept it in my mind and heart for years. Who can resist God's calling? Look to I Corinthians 14:34-35 to see that women are instructed to ask their husbands anything they wish to learn. Then, of course, the pastor is also to be a man dictated by God's commandment.

Since this contains some material that is not suitable for certain ages. I have provided a unique chapter titled "Kiddy Version" so that parents of young children can use this book. Some of this material is blunt and to the point, definitely not for young children. It is my hope and prayer that this will help those parents in this world of top-heavy sexual content. It is more likely that children aged eight or older will understand this chapter better. When presenting this to a young child, not yet ready for a full understanding of virtue, you can tell her that virtue includes things like trust, honor, and truth. You can substitute the phrase "real lady" for a "virtuous woman" so her curiosity will not be aroused. Tell her it is a biblical term that she will understand better as a real lady today. You can also say that virtue is what separates a lady from a woman.

If presented correctly and at the right time, this material can have a profound and lifelong influence on your daughter's life. In matters concerning sex and drugs, telling a girl just to say no is just not enough. Who has not heard of the rebellious child? Rules without understanding will lead to rebellion. We must provide our children motivation that will make them want to abstain from premarital sex as well as drugs to succeed. The more we mystify sex, the more they will want to know. I encourage you to repeat this material at critical intervals because once will never be enough. We all forget things, particularly those things that are presented to us as young children. As time progresses, greater understanding may come with repetition. Don't expect the big talk to be sufficient. I also recommend that adults read this twice to gain a full understanding as well.

The chapters about Sexual Assault and Homosexuality were included because they are a part of the world that we need to be properly taught about. The rest of the chapters outline God's instructions for conducting ourselves. To learn more about how to prevent sexual assault buy my book with the same title: *How to Prevent Sexual Assault.* Our morals and values influence all parts of our lives. Even if you are not a Christian, this material could improve your life (read Appendix A for an example). It is designed to reach people of all age groups as well as both genders. So, if you want a healthier marriage, buy one of these and leave it in a place where your spouse will notice it.

GOD'S PERFECT CREATION

In Genesis 1:26, when God said, "Let us make man in our image," He was not merely referring to man's physical nature. He was also alluding to the fact that He made us sinless as He is. Sin entered the world by one man, not God. God created Adam free from all sin and death.

For all have sinned and come short of the glory of God (Romans 3:23).

Wherefore, as by one-man sin entered into the world, and death by sin (Romans 5:12).

The preceding verses state clearly that to this day, we are all marred by that original sin, and we will all continue to sin until the day we are quickened to meet the Lord.

And the Lord God commanded the man, saying, of every tree of the garden thou mayest freely eat: But of the tree of the knowledge of good and evil, thou shalt not eat of it: for in the day that thou eatest thereof thou shalt surely die (Genesis 2:16-17).

Adam was allowed to eat of any tree in the garden except "the tree of the knowledge of good and evil." He was not forbidden to eat of the tree of life. However, when the first couple disobeyed God, they were put out of the garden, "lest he live forever" (Genesis 3:22-24). In verse 24, God placed cherubim and a flaming sword at the east end of the garden, which turned every way, to keep mankind out lest he should eat of the tree of life.

This started man's search for the lost fountain of youth he has ever sought to regain. Man would never have known death if he had not eaten the forbidden fruit (see I Corinthians 15:21). God forbade him only the singular tree of the knowledge of good and evil.

Let's say you built a beautiful garden. You took great pains to make sure it was unsurpassed by any other. It had a pond with many trails and stonewalls to make it the envy of all who saw it. You planted every fruit-bearing tree you could find from far and wide. You even imported some exotic animals for your garden as well as beautiful birds.

One day, you go away and return to find your garden destroyed by an enemy. All your fences and stonewalls have been torn down. All the beautiful trees have been hewn down. All the animals have been permanently marred and are no longer their lustrous selves. No matter how forgiving you may be, no doubt, this would make you mad. Well, try to imagine how God must have felt when He found His perfect creation, Adam and Eve hiding in the bush because they realized they were naked and ashamed.

No doubt, they were permanently marred just as your garden was. God's and our enemy, Satan, destroyed the garden of Eden to our detriment. To this very day, men and women suffer because of this destruction engineered by the great destroyer, Satan. Do not take on Satan's character by being his follower and ruining the things God has made. For men, that means you are not to destroy one of God's creations by speaking for and taking a maiden's virtue. Learning what God's purpose for women is let's you see that by doing such acts you are obliterating another man's gift from God. Beware of those who

7

destroy anyone or anything, for they are followers of Satan and will bring ruin wherever they go. Make no mistake about it, *God's Feminist Movement* was written to inspire women to be their best and to ultimately realize that the direction the secular feminist movement is going will lead to their destruction.

Let's compare a female giving up her God-given virtue to anyone other than her husband to the original sin of Adam and Eve. If a woman does that, the rest of mankind will not suffer, only her husband. However, like Adam and Eve, she has fallen. Once the deed is done, it cannot ever be undone. Just like Eve was made sinless, every female was made to be a maiden for her husband. She was made pure but is no longer if she gives her purity to another man. Do not be foolish and lose your virtue to a youthful indiscretion. This is another perfect reason to say, "no." When a young man asks, "Why not?" tell him, "Go find your wife and wait for her." Having the motivation to say no is essential; failure is almost certain if you don't.

This material has been included to make you realize what God made us to be. Just as God created Adam and Eve sinless and perfect, He made every girl to grow up to be a virtuous woman. Something flawed cannot become perfect; it has to start out perfect. Every little girl starts out destined to be a Proverbs 31 woman but the same thing that brought Adam and Eve down will prevent her from remaining a Proverbs 31 woman – SIN.

The tokens of her virginity discussed in Deuteronomy 22:15 were no accident. Be not deceived; evolution did not create these tokens in our daughters by any means. Also, they are not found in the animals. Sex before marriage is a very big thing with God as the rest of Chapter 22 demonstrates. Make it a point to ask your daughter how many instances of premarital sex it takes before God considers a girl a whore? Hint, look at verse 22. Use this to teach young girls new respect and value for their virginity. Of course, teaching your sons to value and preserve a maiden will help things a lot. Both sexes are responsible for the state of things today, and it will take both to change it.

Proverbs 22:6 says, "Train up a child in the way he should go: and when he is old, he will not depart from it." Excellence neither happens overnight nor by accident. I was watching a movie where a high school girl was telling her counselor she was a whore. The counselor said she was not. The problem is that many females do not see themselves as whores even though their sexual habits point clearly to the fact that they are. I confirmed this fact with a psychiatrist.

One guy at work was talking about his abilities with the ladies, and I told him, "Any woman who goes to a bar and has sex with a stranger is no lady." On hearing this, a woman standing nearby started crying. On another occasion, as I waited for my car to be serviced, two women were talking about how they were going to pick up someone. I asked them how often they did that, and they replied every week. Then I asked them if they ever picked up the same guy twice; to which they said "never." I asked them how many weeks there are in a year. Next, I asked how many years they had been doing that. They said "ten." After doing the calculations, one woman started to cry and tugged on the other's sleeve. She said, "We whores, we've done 500 guys."

Sin pulls us down from the glory God planned for us. The path to heaven is straight and narrow, (Matthew 7:13-14) as is the road to remaining a lady or gentleman. We have all sinned and come short of the glory of God (Romans 3:23), but we can all still inherit heaven. A lady is not necessarily perfect but virtuous, in many things. The chapter "God's Purpose for Woman" will explain more about why you were given virtue in the first place. Later, you will learn about other virtues to obtain to achieve your utmost. After all, that is the purpose for which this material has been written.

GOD'S DIVINE DESIGN FOR HIS DAUGHTERS

Genesis 2:19-20 tells us God brought all the animals to Adam to be named, but no helpmate was found for him. Don't imagine God was incapable of naming the animals Himself or that He forgot He had not yet made Eve. Adam, being smart enough to name all the animals, undoubtedly realized that if all animals were male and female, there must be a female for him. God wanted to show Adam he was alone, and He was waiting for Adam to figure this out for himself.

Matthew 19:26 says, "With God all things are possible." Clearly, if God wanted to, He could have made Eve from the dust of the ground at the same time and in the same way He made Adam. But God had a purpose for not making Eve at the same time as Adam. He wanted to present Eve as a gift to Adam to fill a need in his life. In Genesis 2:23, Adam called Eve "bone of my bones and flesh of my flesh." Genesis 2:24 says, "They shall be one flesh." If they had been made independent of one another, they would not have been able to cleave together as one.

This becomes very real for us when we examine I Corinthians 11:8-9 and again Genesis 3:12. Adam replies to God, "The woman whom thou gavest to be with me, she gave me of the tree, and I did eat" with an emphasis on the "gavest."

For the man is not of the woman but the woman of the man. Neither was the man created for the woman; but the woman for the man (1 Corinthians 11:8-9).

James 1:17 says, "Every good gift and every perfect gift is from above and cometh down from the Father of lights, with whom is no variableness, neither shadow of turning." If you let sin into your life, you will taint God's gift to your husband just as Satan destroyed man, God's perfect creation. Never allow another to un-wrap your husband's gift. Doing so is like getting a present that someone else opened and then re-taped; no matter what you do, you can't deny the fact it has already been undone. Every time you have sex before your marriage, it makes you less than the woman God made you to be. How wonderful it is to be a perfect gift from God! What beauty God created but how sad that God, most often, must protect us from our very selves.

When God made Eve, He did not take a bone from Adam's foot to tread upon; He took a rib. Genesis 2:20 refers to Eve as a helpmeet. This is what God provided for Adam in Eve. The woman was made from the man, and so, she is a reflection of his glory as the man is the reflection of God's glory.

Ephesians 1:4 tells us we were chosen "before the foundation of the world." God certainly is an awesome God. He knew His children even before He created the world. If you are not a child of God yet, I pray your eyes will be opened so that Luke 10:22 may be accomplished and you will apply Ephesians 1:4 to you. It was not left to chance that we are male or female; our genders were predestined. Evolution is a false theory that is all about chance. However, God never leaves anything to chance. A smarter man than me (Albert Einstein) said: "God does not play dice."

Our identities and personalities depend on whether we were made male or female. As Psalms 139:14 proclaims, "We are fearfully and wonderfully made." See Appendix D for more on this. Since God knew you before the foundation of the world, if you are female, you can expect He intended you to be some man's gift and help meet just as He presented Eve to Adam. Have you ever heard the term, "soul mates"? No one is God's gift to the opposite sex, just to one person.

Let us not forget Matthew 19:26 where Jesus states that with God all things are possible. In Genesis Chapter 24, we see God's involvement in the selection of Isaac's wife. You can be confident that when God said it was not good for the man to be alone, He made a woman to make the man complete. A woman is incomplete without the man as well. I Corinthians 11:11 proclaims that neither is the man without the woman nor is the woman without the man in the Lord. An excellent example of this is a single mother. Single-parent families are incomplete, and the majority are headed by a female. This structure has dire consequences for the children in these households. In today's societies, the feminists propagate a message of independence for women. However, those teachings are direct contradictions to God's designs for humanity. The feminists say marriage is oppressive, but they are incorrect. Marriage completes God's purpose for both man and woman.

Being a woman is about what you can do and not what you are due. Do everything for the glory of God, not womankind as the secular feminist would have you believe. I heard a pastor on the radio say, "Submission is simply the way you live your life." Submit to Christ, and He will set you free from Satan's deceit.

Every time Satan puts his mark on what God has created, it becomes flawed, worth less (that's a play on words). The first and best example of this is when he crept into the garden and got man cast out. The feminists are continuing that. 1Peter 5:8 says, "Be sober, be vigilant; because your adversary the devil, as a roaring lion, walketh about, seeking whom he may devour." James 1:13, tells us that God cannot tempt us. Only Satan tells us, "If it feels good, do it," or "It's just sex." Something that can take your life or create life can never be reduced to just sex. Whenever we listen to the subtle lies of Satan, we are brought down from the perfect position God created us for (Romans 5:12). Satan cannot cheat us of heaven, but he can still rob us. Just as there are different degrees of punishment in hell, there are different rewards in heaven (Deuteronomy 32:22 and Matthew 5:19). There are also least and greatest in the kingdom of heaven, which is evident in Luke 7:28.

When Satan was thrown from heaven (Revelation 12:9-12) the angels said, "Woe to the inhabitants of the earth." Surely, nothing good can befall a man married to a woman who has destroyed God's gift to him with sin. She has turned God's gift into woe-man. Nor is an evil man a blessing to his wife either.

Do not make the mistake of letting false pride come into your heart through anything I have said or will say. God made a woman as His gift to a man. If you let the sin of premarital sex into your life, you will destroy God's gift, to your husband just like Adam and Eve ruined mankind, God's perfect creation. You will become a cheap imitation like tinkling brass. There are no exceptions for sin for men either.

WHAT GOD DOES NOT WANT FROM HIS DAUGHTERS?

I titled this book *God's Feminist Movement* because I've met and heard of many Christian women who also call themselves feminists. I hope and pray this book opens their eyes to the danger they expose their souls to by associating with feminists.

"Let not thine heart envy sinners: but be thou in the fear of the LORD all the day long" (Proverbs 23:17). As I Corinthians 3:8 says, "Every man shall receive his own reward according to his own labor."

The feminists' stance on abortion is readily apparent. Clearly, they confuse teenagers with grown women. They feel teenage girls have the right to make their own decisions. I ask myself and wish you would do the same: "What Christian would support people who fight militantly for abortions." More importantly, what will God say when they get to the pearly gates? I am sure God does not feel it is a choice but a life. Perhaps, if the other feminists were genuinely working for the good of women, they would teach their followers that sex is important and not merely a tool to be used.

Hitler may have lost the war, but it seems he won one battle. You see, under Hitler's regime if you were handicapped or not an essential worker, you were killed. Today, if you are merely inconvenienced, you get an abortion. Why do you think the government subsidizes/pays for abortions? The only answer I can think of is – it is cheaper than welfare.

The feminists also openly embrace lesbians. Do you realize that those who turn God's truth into lies will not inherit heaven? We are talking about God's natural order of the man for woman. What will God do to those who throw their voices in with lesbians? Far be it for me to say but I sincerely pray you turn from this folly. See Proverbs 17:15 for more on this.

The feminists have fought diligently for years to get women into combat and are not about to let a few setbacks stop them. They have managed to enable women to be fighter pilots. Now women can volunteer for combat positions. There have been reports on the news that women may have to register for the selective service just like their male counterparts. If the draft is reenacted woman may be selected as well. See what happens when you let the feminists run unchecked. War makes big, strong men cry for their mommas in their sleep. Many men come back suffering from posttraumatic stress disorder (PTSD). You see, war is, indeed, hell. So, face the fact ladies, you will suffer far worse than men do from PTSD in wars. Then, you will also be among the amputees. If you do not have a clue what will happen to you should you be captured, you will, once you read the chapter on Preventing Sexual Assault.

I recently read that the Veterans Administration is going to review more than one and a half million claims of (PTSD). What makes you think women can handle war better than men? I neither want to get into a long debate about psychology nor am I sexist but women are more prone to neurotic responses to stress whether self-induced or external. If a mouse runs across the floor, a woman is more likely than a man to jump on a chair and freak out. When a bee flies in a woman's bonnet, she flips out well after it has gone.

Do you want a few women to speak for you and lead you down this path to war? If not, you had better take steps to ensure they know you oppose them. You had better join the growing anti-feminist movement! Particularly, I think you had better let your congressmen know your true feelings about women in combat. Even if feminist's numbers are falling, they are not out of the fight and are still a strong lobbying force.

So ought men to love their wives as their own bodies. He that loveth his (God) loveth himself. For no man ever yet hated his own flesh: but nourisheth and cherisheth it, even as the Lord the church. Nevertheless let every one of you in particular so love his wife even as himself: and the wife see that she reverence her husband (Ephesians 5:28-29; 33).

In this passage, God instructs men to love their wives as themselves. Everything a husband expects of his wife, she is due to receive from him. Women are also due honor and respect. It would be hypocritical to expect something from your spouse without expecting to give the same in return. As an example, the man is instructed to converse with his wife in the same fashion that he would expect from her. It is important to remember the man is the head of the home just as God is the head of the man. A woman is commanded to reverence her husband; this is her ministry to him. The man has a higher authority to which He must answer (God). A woman should be able to trust her husband always, also, so their marriage is not spoiled because of him either. Indeed, there is no exception for either sex from adultery or sinning against their spouses. Also abstain from all appearance of evil as 1 Timothy 5:22 warns us. This will prevent any jealousy creeping into your spouse's heart.

Do you still believe you are not equal to men or are you striving to obtain superiority over them? God had equality in mind for men and women all along. Somewhere along the way, both sexes have gotten lost. Satan is stirring up women to think they are not equal to men. He is lying just as he did to Eve in the garden. For just as sin came into the world and destroyed God's creation if a woman lets premarital sex into her life, God's gift to her husband is tainted. She will no longer be a helpmate but woe-man. Sir Walter Raleigh started the tradition of a man laying his coat over a puddle. In this world of, "It's just sex." I wonder if he would consider it worth the price of the cleaning bill for a woman of today; a bitter pill perhaps, but not if you are walking on the right path.

God does not view women as inferior to the men as the feminists lead you to believe. "There is neither Jew nor Greek; there is neither bond nor free, there is neither male nor female: for ye are all one in Christ Jesus" (Galatians 3:28). This scripture does not mean women are to perform the roles of men or men are to do the work of women. Look for some scriptures that define a man's responsibilities to his wife and family. Did you find any that allow men to shrink from their responsibilities? Is it appropriate for either sex to desire to do the other's roles?

When Satan crept into the garden, he chose the form of a serpent. Satan uses many lies and disguises to pull us down. Today, he has a new lie, which is that a woman is lifted up if she is made equal to a man. Nowhere does the Bible say that a man can be worth more than or even an amount equal to rubies. On the contrary, a truly virtuous woman's worth is far above rubies. That does not make her head over the man ever. She will never attempt to usurp authority over the man (I Timothy 2:12).

Do not let Satan fool you into pursuing a false equality. The truth is that once again, Satan has cheated us. The woman is being deceived in that she is being pulled down. If a woman does achieve equality with a man, she becomes worth less. The man who ends up with her will be robbed of a tremendous precious jewel. If you believe that liberating yourself is lifting you up, you have been fooled. You have actually brought yourself down.

Women do need to be liberated – from the lies of the Devil. Enroll yourself in God's Feminist Movement and avoid Satan's Feminist Movement. It has been said that there will never be an end to the battle of the sexes because there is too much fraternizing with the Enemy.[2] The scriptures proclaim that woman was not put here to do battle with men but to do just the opposite. You will begin to see this as you read more. Anything that puts women against men is not the work of God but of Satan. Avoid the devices of Satan.

SILVER PALACE

We have a little sister, and she hath no breasts: what shall we do for our sister in the day when she shall be spoken for? If she be a wall, we will build upon her a palace of silver: and if she be a door, we will inclose her with boards of cedar (Song of Solomon 8:8-9).

Although elusive, the interpretation of this passage is quite simple and basic. Here, two siblings are discussing their little sister. We know this girl is prepubescent because she has no breasts. However, as a girl blossoms into a young lady, the boys who notice this shall speak for her virtue by tempting her with the lust of their youth. Some mistakenly think that the day their little sisters are spoken for is their wedding day. Undoubtedly, every girl has had her virtue spoken for long before her wedding day even back in biblical times. It says right here in the preceding verse that this will happen. That doesn't make it right but be certain; it will happen before her marriage. Parents need to educate their daughters for that day and teach their sons that it is not their right to speak for a girl's virtue.

What does comparing her to a wall or a door mean? If an invading force wanted to pillage a city and they came to a wall, they would find it unyielding, and it would be impossible to complete their invasion. Certainly, they would go to a door since it would yield to them. This same principle of the door and wall applies to the little girl when her virtue is spoken for. Be sure she will not figure out why she needs to be a wall on her own.

Proverbs 29:15 says, "The rod and reproof give wisdom: but a child left to himself bringeth his mother to shame." Children left to their own devices will run astray every time.

What should her brothers do for their sister? If she is a wall, unyielding to the lustful advances of the invading young boys, they will build a palace of silver around her. She certainly will be worthy of having a silver palace built upon her. However, if she yields as a door to the lust of her youth, she will be enclosed with boards of cedar. In other words, she will be prevented from sinning (fornicating). Ask a young man, who is more valuable: a young lady who owns a silver palace or one who has to live in a cedar box? Then ask him which one he would prefer to marry. Today, a girl's brothers should take on the responsibility for guarding their little sister's purity.

Regarding this specific interpretation of Song of Solomon 8:8-9: this book has received more varied interpretations than any other book in the Bible.[3] Many interpret this scripture as an allegory with the girl being considered as the church. However, the text itself does not indicate that we should interpret this book any differently than any other Bible book.[4] Others interpret it literally, historically, and grammatically as all the other books are, which is the favored version by your author. I believe it is most useful in providing yet another inspiration for a girl to grow up righteous as God created/intended her to. And I am firmly convinced that God never tries to hide His truth from us with stories that their real meanings need to be guessed. Consider II Timothy 3:16, "All scripture is given by inspiration of God, and is profitable for doctrine, for reproof, for correction, for instruction in righteousness."

Talk to your daughter while young about retaining her virtue until she marries. What chance is there that she will care to if you do not show her you care? Give her many good reasons to do so. Repeat the reasons at appropriate intervals since we all forget things at one time or another. Then when a boy asks: "Why not?" she will have good cause to say "no." The correct question is "Why should I?" "Why not?" is not an appropriate question for him to be asking. After all, he is not her husband.

It would also help to teach young men that when they are on dates, the girls they are holding could eventually become other men's wives. Also, remind them that someone else is out with their future wives.

Do not wait until your daughter is fully developed to start speaking to her about her virtue. These brothers in the Song of Solomon knew that the boys would speak for their sister's virtue. Waiting until her wedding day would be far past this event in her life and be utterly useless. I Corinthians 7 clearly commands women not to be walls to their husbands. As we shall see, any delay could have cost a girl her life in biblical times.

Back in biblical times, some men would marry women just to have sex. That is evidence of the type of women who existed back then; men had to marry them to get sex. After marriage and sex, the man would say the woman was not a virgin so he could put her away by divorce. That was the purpose of securing the proof of her virginity mentioned in Deuteronomy 22. However, if it was found to be true, she was to be taken to her father's door and stoned. This law certainly inspired sexual purity before marriage and encouraged parents to teach their daughters to abstain before marriage.

With God, it is hard to discern if the death of the flesh is the same as that of the spirit. Even today, more than ever; parents should still influence their children's lives because God never changes.

A woman who was being divorced by her husband told me he just married her to have sex with her. What a testimony to this woman's character it is that he had to marry her first. Certainly, this is what God wants from His daughters of today. Virtue is not a small thing with God, evident by His sign that He put in His daughters' bodies. Because everyone else is doing it, today, will not help you. Beware: God's laws are never changing because He is a rock on which we can always stand. The secular feminists will never move nor change Him. Amen!

In 1974, my grandfather died. One of his brothers came from Grand Manan, an island in Canada, to attend the funeral. He invited us to return with him to visit Grand Manan for a couple of weeks, which we accepted. This gave me the chance to see where my grandfather had grown up and to learn things about him that I had never known before. Since he was born around the turn of the 20th century, it was fascinating to hear about life back then.

One interesting thing I learned was how my grandfather and his brother had to keep after their sister to enclose her in those proverbial boards of cedar. Her birth name was Louise. We all called her Lou-Lou. Believe me when I say the name fit. They have all since gone on to meet the Lord, and I am pretty sure even He had a hard time straightening her out. It was touching to hear how they both had taken care of their sister, something rarely heard about even in the '70s. Today it is all *zoom-zoom* and *boom-boom*, and too many don't care if it's their sister or not.

GOD'S LITTLE CHILDREN

Matthew 18:10 tells us of the angels of the little ones and how they always behold the face of God. Mark 9:42 and Luke 17:2 talk about the consequences of offending one of these little ones who believe in Jesus. We are warned that it is better for a millstone to be hung about the offender's neck and the person be cast into the sea.

In Luke 20:34-36 and Mathew 12:25, Jesus informs the Sadducees that those who enter heaven are not given in marriage and are now equal to the heavenly angels. Hebrews 2:7 proves that God did make mankind a little lower than the angels, who reinforces the statement, "are now equal to the heavenly angels." I look forward to that day when I become equal with the angels and engage in the same work as them. On my headstone I want it printed, "Finally! I have become equal with the angels." I hope you discover as I did a long time ago that Satan has no one to stop us from doing as much of the angels' work in this world before we die as we can. Follow me! Don't be afraid to act as an angel of the little ones as I mentioned above.

James 4:17 says "Therefore to him that knoweth to do good, and doeth it not to him it is sin." If you have the opportunity to do good for one of God's little children and you do not, you have sinned against them. Their angels will testify against you before God's throne; It won't matter if you are or are not their parent. Proverbs 3:27 may be referring to money but I could not help but think of James 4:17 when I first read it; I also apply it to God's children. Withhold not good from them to whom it is due, when it is in the power of thine hand to do it (Proverbs 3:27). I am not necessarily advising you to go looking for an opportunity.

I just want you to recognize when it comes along and not be afraid to seize the opportunity. And note, it does not mean you should give the children lickings if they are not yours. Instead, admonish and instruct them and/or tell their parents. Wording your instructions as a question will help avoid conflict. I do not believe God puts any limitations on his believers from doing good for others especially our church family. This is evident in Galatians 6:10. Why bother with Sunday school for them then if it is forbidden to teach other people's children? That sounds like a great opportunity to me.

As we have therefore, let us do good unto all men, especially unto them who are of the household of faith (Galatians 6: 10).

I once had a friend with a little daughter named Julie. She used to ask me why I did the things for her that I did. I told her God told me to do it even though she was not mine and that there were not enough ladies in the world. Lastly, I said to her that if everyone in her life would influence her as I did, she could not fail to become a godly woman. I have written this out of my great desire to provide some guidance for the rest of the Julies in the world.

Many times, I have heard it said to respect your elders. The closest to this that I can find in the Bible is I Peter 5: 5: "Likewise, ye younger, submit your selves unto the elder." The "younger" in this context, not only refers to young children but those young in the faith and led by the elders and pastors. God did not command the "younger" to submit to the authority and instructions of their elders to be neglected, misled or abused by them. Following James 4:17 can get you into a lot of trouble if you are not very, very careful. It requires a lot of tact and diplomacy even then, you will run into trouble. Use common sense, for only fools rush in. The type of person mentioned in Proverbs 17:13 who repays good with evil is a fool who has an evil heart. This is one reason why following James 4:17 may cause grief. When God said the world would hate us, He was not wrong, in the least.

You must walk to the beat of a different drummer when you decide to live for Christ. If the world does not hate you, perhaps, you are not living right. A woman once told me there was no such thing as unconditional love. To which I asked her: "How many years have you been going to church?" I told her she had not learned a thing. Children are an excellent example of unconditional love; they will love you pretty much with no strings attached. They do not see or mention your faults. Rest assured they want your presence in their lives over any present you can give. It is just about the closest you can get in this world to God's unconditional love. Sad to say, you will never find a spouse like that. That explains a lot about why I love children so much. Possibly, that's why Jesus also did.

The Importance of Family to God's Little Ones

Given the divorce rate today, there are lots of stepchildren in the world. If you have stepchildren, you should raise them with the same love and discipline you would give to your own; they come along with the territory. I share this because I know of one man who was to marry a woman with four children. He thought he could fool God and get away with not doing his duties to his future wife's children. It ended up that the marriage was delayed once he realized his responsibilities.

Now that you have received this knowledge of the truth, you cannot escape your responsibility to do what's right for God's little children as James 4:17 instructs. "Be not deceived God is not mocked" (Galatians 6:7). You cannot shrink back from this and escape for God knows all the thoughts of our hearts (Hebrews 4:12).

Compared with continuously married parents, single parents are less emotionally supportive of their children, have fewer rules yet dispense harsher discipline, and provide less supervision; stepparents spend less time with children and offer less positive response and encouragement (Astone & McLanahan, 1991; McLanahan & Sandefur, 1994; Thomson, McLanahan, & Curtin, 1992). It is time for stepparents to step up and be involved in the children's lives they have accepted into their world. Go big or go home as they say.

The ones who suffer most in a divorce are the children. Children who grow up with two married parents tend to fare better than others (The Future of Children. 2005). Alcohol and drug addictions' makes for a violent home life for children. Be very careful in your selection of a spouse. The destruction of the family is the work of Satan. The family is one more thing God has created that the Devil is destroying. Applying God's Feminist Movement to your life will help liberate your family from Satan's attacks on it.

If you deliberately sabotage your marriage, as the worldly feminists have instructed you, be aware that you will stand before God's throne and answer for every negative consequence your actions have caused in your children's lives. Swallow your pride and make amends if you can to preserve your marriage. Forget about no-fault divorce; it will not help you when you stand before God's throne.

Dangers of Feeding God's Little One's Unhealthy Foods

Children who eat more than 12 hot dogs per month have nine times the average risk of developing childhood leukemia, a University of Southern California epidemiologist reports in a cancer research journal. Two other reports in the same issue of Cancer Causes and Control also suggest that children born to mothers who eat, at least, one hot dog per week during pregnancy have double the normal risk of developing brain tumors as do children whose fathers ate hot dogs before conception. The findings, which already are generating a great deal of controversy and concern, could help explain why the incidence of childhood leukemia and brain tumors has been increasing over the last two decades, say the researchers, led by USC epidemiologist Dr. John Peters.[5]

The American Institute for Cancer Research (AICR) and the World Cancer Research Fund found that consuming just 50 grams of processed meat (think one hot dog) daily increases the risk of colorectal cancer, on average, by 21 percent. How could hot dogs cause cancer? Hot dogs contain nitrites, which are used as preservatives and to combat botulism. During the cooking, nitrites combine with amines naturally present in meat to form carcinogenic N-nitroso compounds. It is also suspected that nitrites combine with amines in the stomach to form N- nitroso compounds. These compounds are known carcinogens and have been associated with cancer of the oral cavity, urinary bladder, esophagus, stomach, and brain.

Not all hot dogs on the market contain nitrites. Because of modern refrigeration, nitrites are now used more for the red color they produce (which is associated with freshness) than for preservation. Nitrite-free hot dogs have a brownish color that has limited their popularity among consumers. When cooked, nitrate-free hot dogs are perfectly safe and healthy. I know of one child who would eat nothing but hot dogs, morning, noon, and night. Well, not in the morning of course but he loved them. Having the above information in my heart, I could not keep from telling his parents about the chance of him getting leukemia. He resisted his parents so much; they had to give him the option of nothing or the "other meat" on his plate. It was but two weeks, and he was telling his parents how much better he felt. The world thinks that denying a child the nourishment of a meal and thereby inflicting the pain of hunger is equal to that of a licking. Hopefully, this convinces you of the danger of that folly to a child. Such foolishness is far crueler than a thrashing.

Acne is the dread of all teenagers so sharing this is my example of doing something good for God's children. I remember watching a health film in the fifth grade about preventing acne. The point made was that the oil, which produces pimples does not go anywhere. Therefore, even if you were not going anywhere, you needed to wash frequently throughout the day, precisely three times. Wash once in the morning, of course, once again after coming home from school and again before going to bed. Guys if you are reading this there is nothing feminine about washing your face. The most important thing they stressed was that you were to wash three times; each time using water as hot as you could stand then rinse with cold water. The hot water opens up your pores to allow you to scrub deeper with each successive washing. The cold water closes the pores again preventing more dirt and oil from clogging them up, which is what causes pimples in the first place. I told this to the young lady mentioned in Appendix A, and she never had a single pimple.

KIDDY VERSION

God made the earth and everything on it in six days. On the seventh day, He rested. Genesis 2:19-20 tells us that God brought all the animals to Adam to be named, but no helpmate was found for him. Don't imagine for one moment that God was incapable of naming the animals Himself. Also, He did not forget Eve was not yet created. Adam, being smart enough to name all the animals, undoubtedly realized that if all animals were male and female, there should be a female for him. God wanted to show Adam that he was alone. He was waiting for Adam to figure this out for himself.

God made Adam and Eve perfect and without sin (Romans 5:12). Just as the Bible says, they sinned and were cast out of the garden. The same way God made Eve without sin when He presented her to Adam, He created you to grow up to be a lady. It is true that we all do wrong things occasionally, but if you keep doing the same wrong things without learning not to do them, it is unlikely you will grow up to be a lady as God made you to be. You will need to be honorable to be a lady.

God has a purpose for everything He has ever done. In his great wisdom, He made the ocean first and then all the fish in it, rather than making the fish first then having to keep them all in tanks until He made the ocean. It was much easier. "With God all things are possible" (Matthew 19:26).

Clearly, if God wanted to, He could have made Eve from the dust of the ground at the same time and in the same way He created Adam. God had a reason and a purpose for not making Eve at the same time as Adam. He wanted to present Eve as a gift to Adam to fill a need in his life. James 1:17 says that every good and perfect gift is from above and comes down from God. God knew you even before He made the world. He wants to present you as a perfect gift to someone also. So, if you want to grow up to be a gift from God, you must be good and follow all His rules. You want to grow up to be a real lady because ladies are worth far more than rubies.

If you want to grow up to be a lady, you have to start out as a little lady. Do not worry about the rules for the grown-up ladies just work on being a little lady for now. Know that you cannot grow into a lady overnight; it takes time and work. God had a plan for Eve, and He has a plan for you too. He knew you before the foundation of the world (Ephesians 1:4). It was part of His plan that you are a girl. He also picked out your parents. We honor our parents by the way we talk to them and by doing what they say. Disobeying them is like saying that God made a bad choice in selecting who would be your parents.

You are the best thing Mom and Dad can give the world. We want you to be the best you can be. This does not mean you have to be the best at everything but just to do your best in all things. You are loved by both us and God. We wish only good for you and always want to be proud of you. We want you to be a little girl and have as much fun as you can because someday, little girls must grow up. Nothing is wrong with having fun; being a lady does not mean you cannot enjoy life.

From Proverbs 11:16, we learn that a gracious woman retains honor. Being gracious is important. It means to be kind. It is not kind to scream when we do not get our own ways. That means no temper tantrums, and you should go to bed when Mom and Dad say to.

Little ladies do what their parents tell them to do and are reliable. Ladies and Gentlemen never deliberately hurt anyone's feelings. This subtracts from people's lives and is not from God.

Who can find a virtuous woman? For her price is far above rubies (Proverbs 31:10).

Just as Adam and Eve were created sinless, I believe every girl born was given everything she needs to become a virtuous woman. It is sin that will keep her from growing into a godly woman. Even back in Old Testament times, not every little girl grew up to be a virtuous woman. Hence the question, "Who can find a virtuous woman?" Every little girl eventually grows up to be a woman but not all become ladies for God. Virtue is not only for the rich, and it cannot be bought. Virtue includes things like being trustworthy, honorable, and truthful. God gives virtue to every female when she is born. He has destined His daughters to grow up as Proverbs 31 women. The same thing that pulled down God's perfect creation prevents girls from achieving God's designs for them. SIN.

A flawless ruby is worth more than a diamond. "For her price is far above rubies," means that she is priceless. Be good, and when Prince Charming comes along, he will recognize you for your true worth. I believe that God made all little girls to be Proverbs 31 women when they grow up, just as God created man in His image – sinless (Romans 5:12). Sin will prevent a girl from blossoming into the beautiful godly woman God designed her to be. There are many ways to be rich other than to have money. A man married to a real lady is wealthy beyond imagination. The love between a good wife and a good husband is one of these ways.

Imagine you have been invited to a grand ball like the one Cinderella went to. This ball was held for the Prince to find a wife. You are instructed to come as you are, but you will need to provide your gown size because one will be provided for you when you arrive. You arrive on the evening of the big day to find that you are one of one hundred females that were invited. Each of you are given a number and told that it is also the number of your gown. You are also advised that only eighty- eight fellers were invited. They will not know who goes with which gown but the guys will get to pick out his partner for the night by choosing which dress he likes.

They have been warned to examine the gowns carefully as twelve of them have been ripped; torn; have holes in them and basically have been abused. There were more than enough costumes to choose from so the abused ones were not desirable nor selected. The twelve girls that these gowns represent will be sent home from the ball immediately after the selection process is over. The number of boys to girls is never equal. Eventually when young men begin to search for a wife, they can be very selective.

A VIRTUOUS WOMAN

Precisely what is a virtuous woman?

Who can find a virtuous woman? for her price is far above rubies? (Proverbs 31:10).

As mentioned earlier, even in the Old Testament times, not every little girl grew up to be a virtuous woman. Hence the question, "Who can find a virtuous woman?" But if a woman is God's gift to man, how can this be? "SIN" Spell it out loud. What is in the middle of the word "sin"? "I." am. Being a virtuous woman requires many things, getting a young girl to retain her virtue is an excellent start in the right direction. Giving a girl a sense of self-worth that is far above rubies will do just that.

"Her price is far above rubies," means that a virtuous woman is priceless. When a ruby is flawless, it's more valuable than a diamond.[6] Who said diamonds are a girl's best friend? An expert told me that flawless rubies do exist, but you will spend a lifetime finding one. Marring a Proverbs 31 woman is like finding a flawless ruby.

Every little girl eventually grows up to be a woman, but not all become ladies for God. Statistically, the current methods parents are choosing do not seem to be working. Time to try new techniques.

This is not a put-down, but the secular feminists will have you believe that you are special just because you are a female. Young girls taught this lie are most likely destined for failure because they will believe everything, they do is OK. But that's not so because it takes work to retain the worth of "far above rubies." I witnessed a mother tell her daughter she was a precious jewel after she was very rude to a playmate.

Substituting "real lady" for a virtuous woman is a good way to dodge a young child's curiosity. If you do not feel she is ready to know exactly what this aspect of virtue is. This strategy also works if you are too embarrassed to tell her about sex just yet. Tell her that a virtuous woman is a biblical term for what we know today as a real lady. When a 3-year-old asks where babies come from, you wouldn't tell them the truth now, would you?

This scriptural comparison declares a woman of virtue as something of far greater value. Sin is a flaw. If we let sin into our lives, we become flawed. If a young girl allows sin into her life and loses her virtue, she is flawed and worth less. She will become just like what Soft Cell sings in their song "Tainted Love."

The best thing to do is to instill a desire that will make her want to hold on to her virtue until her wedding night. I will not make an apology for God's Word, but your iniquity will be before you on your wedding night. As Jeremiah 2:22 states, "'For though thou wash thee with nitre, and take thee much soap, yet thine iniquity is marked before me,' saith the Lord God."

A young woman saving her virtue for her future husband will secure her husband's blessing and favor from God. It is a sure sign of her benefit to her husband and that she will make a good wife. The same applies to a man. God commands him to save himself as a blessing to his wife.

All too often I have seen young women fall for lack of a good reason to abstain from premarital sex. Satan can certainly capitalize on that weakness. Therefore, it is essential for young women to know why they should not have sex before marriage and that someone else cares. Show your daughter you care by giving her a ruby that will inspire her to remember her true worth, which is far above rubies. That would be a promise ring to the next level.

It is my thinking that something tangible like a ruby will make abstinence more important to a young lady. It will also serve as a continual reminder of her value. Lastly but not the least of my reasoning is that I believe giving her a ruby will demonstrate how much you care as parents. Proverbs 31 scriptures are still true without them being given a ruby though. One mother told me she did not plan on spending any time instructing her daughter. I told her "You should plan on failing." It is a reflection of the quality of your parenting when your daughter walks down the aisle. It is time for parents to own up to this.

When you present your daughter with a ruby necklace, say to her, "Wear this ruby as a reminder of the value God has for you. Sin will flaw you just as this ruby is." This may seem very negative, but if you were not told sex was bad before marriage, you would not have abstained either. If you are never made aware of the sin in your life, you will never know to repent and ask Jesus into your life. So why should it be any different with sex?

If your daughter is old enough, you could tell her to wear her ruby necklace whenever she is out on a date. If her date asks, "Why not?" She will have an inescapable answer: "I am flawless and will remain so until my marriage to my future husband." She could also say, "I will not flaw myself like this ruby." She could say this without the ruby, but its presence will be a good reminder of the consequences of premarital sex in the heat of the moment. If you are dealing with this issue too late in your daughter's life, then tell her to say, "This ruby represents the value God made me for, and I am going to fulfill His glory."

Virtue is not only for the rich. As a matter of fact, no one can buy it. God gives virtue to every female when she is born. He has destined His daughters to grow up as Proverbs 31 women. The challenge is getting them to hold on to their virtue until their wedding nights.

Becoming a Proverbs 31 woman requires many things but retaining the virtue God gives to each girl when she is born is an excellent foundation to build upon. Just as Adam and Eve were created sinless, every girl is born with everything she needs to become a virtuous woman. It is sin that will keep her from growing into a Godly woman.

The heart of her husband doth safely trust in her, so that he shall have no need of spoil (Proverbs 31:11).

A real lady would never let more than one man at a time have her attention or affections in any way. Her husband will have faith in her that she will not spoil their marriage. She will also tend to his business in his absence so he shall lose nothing. A wise woman will not spoil anything of her husband's especially herself before or during their marriage.

She will do him good and not evil all the days of her life. Her husband is known in the gates, when he sitteth among the elders of the land (Proverbs 31:12, 23).

A virtuous woman will lift up her husband and do only good things for him all of her days. All of a person's days begin on the day she was born until the day she dies. Look at a tombstone for a numeration of all of that person's days. What can you think of that fits the description of doing good, and not evil?

Playing cruel games is evil, and a wise woman will flee from anyone who teaches to do so. Of course, this discussion of "all of her days" includes the days she lives before her marriage as well as those after.

Saving her virtue for her future husband is the first good thing a woman can do for her husband. This is also the first and best indication of her love for him even if she has not met him yet. Chances are he is out there somewhere. If she did not love him, would she marry him?

He will be known simply by her reputation (Pro 31:23). She will give him good words, not bad ones. She will never distort her husband's words or be a manipulator. That does not mean she cannot share her feelings, negative thoughts or dissatisfactions. Just don't bombard him with the burdens of your day the moment he comes home from work. Do not scream at your husband unless there is a fire or someone is hurting you. What other reason is there to yell? As Proverbs 15:1 says, "A soft answer turneth away wrath, but grievous words stir up anger." A virtuous woman will express her thoughts and feelings to her husband with grace.

That does not mean she cannot talk to her husband as the other feminists would have you believe. It states she should speak to her husband with kind words and a godly man will appreciate her for it.

If any man among you seem to be religious, and bridleth not his tongue, but deceiveth his own heart, this man's religion is vain (James 1:26).

"O generation of vipers, how can ye, being evil, speak good things? For out of the abundance of the heart the mouth speaketh" (Matthew 12:34). Do you want to know a person's heart? Listen to his/her words. Beware of habitual and masterful liars!

Baby girls have larger communication centers and emotional memory centers in their brains than boys do at birth. Their brains will also mature two years earlier than boys. Girls are more talkative than the boys; this is why females become fast friends and generally only engage in conversations with these friends. Boys are more aggressive and action-oriented in their friendships. Females also display aggression, but it is usually only verbal. Beware of being critical of your husbands.

Even so the tongue is a little member, and boasteth great things. Behold, how great a matter a little fire kindleth! 6 And the tongue is a fire, a world of iniquity: so is the tongue among our members, that it defileth the whole body, and setteth on fire the course of nature; and it is set on fire of hell (James 3: 5).

She seeketh wool, and flax, and worketh willingly with her hands. She considereth a field, and buyeth it: with the fruit of her hands, she planteth a vineyard (Proverbs 31:13, 16).

Seeking wool and flax means that she is industrious in her duties. She applies herself to a woman's proper business and does not try to do men's work. She does not coerce her husband to do a woman's job. The "fruits of her hands" refer to her work, and she works "willingly." She takes pleasure in her job and does not want to quit to loaf.

She is dependable with money. This is evident when she considers a field before buying it to determine if it will benefit her family. Her consideration also proves she is not impulsive and will never do anything without forethought.

"She planteth a vineyard" makes one wonder where the expression "a woman's place is in the home" came from. Planting a vineyard would seem to be equivalent to owning a business. Not everyone can own his or her own business. Likewise, not every woman can plant a vineyard. In today's society, it is becoming increasingly difficult to live on one income. A virtuous woman today is willing to share in the financial burden of the family without complaining about spending her money. Starting daycare is a good way to be home with your children and help with the expenses of a family. She is like the merchant's ships; she bringeth her food from afar (Proverbs 31:14).

She will bring variety into the lives of her family by getting her food from distant markets. In today's world that is not as difficult as it was for our biblical sisters. She will also keep her life from getting into a rut and bring joy and variety into her husband's life in all things. She recognizes the need for diversity in her family's entertainment as well as their food.

She riseth also while it is yet night, and giveth meat to her household and a portion to her maidens (Proverbs 31:15).

She will rise before her family and prepare the morning meal for all those who are under her roof. She knows that it is the most important meal of her household's day. It is called breakfast because that is what it does – breaks the nights fast. Giving a portion to her maidens shows she thinks about the needs of others.

She girdeth her loins with strength, and strengtheneth her arms (Proverbs 31:17).

The above verse does not necessarily mean she increases her physical strength by working out. A virtuous woman will not take advantage of her husband's love by letting herself get out of shape. From my personal observation, the first thing most women do after a divorce is to work out. They know no one wants them in their current physical shape. Just because there is more to love does not mean your husband is going to love you that much more.

As the woman is the weaker vessel, I believe here, she strengthens herself with wisdom and grace. Proverbs 24:5 tells us that a wise man is strong and a man of knowledge increases strength. That is the same wisdom spoken of in Proverbs 3. Wisdom is more precious than rubies: and all the things you can desire cannot compare (vs. 15). Wisdom will bring the bearer a long life, riches, and honor (vs. 16). Proverbs 1:22 states that fools hate knowledge. Gain understanding and liberate yourself from feminist lies. By the time many women who follow them do the best part of their lives have passed.

She perceiveth that her merchandise is good: her candle goeth not out by night. She layeth her hands to the spindle, and her hands hold the distaff (Proverbs 31:18 19).

She is careful not to waste time. She lengthens her day by doing things by candlelight such as the spinning mentioned. By perceiving her merchandise, she knows her worth and is confident in herself because her works are excellent. She will not require praise to accomplish this. A kind word of encouragement and recommendation once in a while is not out of line either.

She eateth not the bread of idleness by wasting time or engaging in idle gossip (vs. 27b). She raises her children well by looking to their ways (vs. 27a). This chapter is an excellent example of a mother's instructions to her children. It is actually the teachings King Lemuel's mother gave him.

She is not afraid of the snow for her household: for all her household are clothed with scarlet (Proverbs 31:21).

The snow here indicates storms in her future. Tragedy and change are parts of everyone's life. Yet, the virtuous woman is emotionally secure and can weather all storms in whatever fashion they do come. Her household is clothed with scarlet because she has saved in preparation for that day. The tale of Abigail in 1 Samuel 25 is a beautiful example of a godly woman; it also explains what rewards a good woman can receive. Verse 3 describes Abigail as a woman full of understanding and a beautiful countenance. She is full of common sense. While her husband, Nabal, was churlish and evil in his doings.

David sent ten young men to Nabal with instructions to request something of him in return for their treatment at Carmel (vs. 5–9). Nabal ridiculed them and sent them away empty-handed (vs. 11-12). His action incited David, and he told four hundred of his men to put on their swords (vs. 13).

Proverbs 17:13 says, "Whoso rewardeth evil for good; evil shall not depart from his house." David said, "Surely in vain have I kept all that this fellow hath in the wilderness, so that nothing was missed of all that pertained unto him: and he hath requited me evil for good (vs. 23)."

One of David's young men told Abigail that evil was determined against her husband and his entire household (vs. 17). Abigail hastily put together some food and laid it on asses. She sent her servants ahead of her to David (v. 14-20). When she met David herself, she fell before him on her face, and persuaded him not to kill her household (v. 24-31). David said, "And blessed be thy advice, and blessed be thou, which hast kept me this day from coming to shed blood, and from avenging myself with mine own hand" (v. 33). "So, David received of her hand that which she had brought him, and said unto her, go up in peace to thine house, see, I have hearkened to thy person" (vs. 35).

Nabal's very name means "fool" and Abigail told David "as his name is, so is he" (vs. 25). Nabal did not deserve such a virtuous wife. But she did what she had to because a good wife does only good to her husband all of her days. When Abigail told Nabal what had happened with David, his heart died within him, and he became as a stone (vs. 37). About ten days later, the Lord smote Nabal, and he died of a heart attack. When David heard that Nabal had died, he sent for Abigail to take her as his wife (vs. 39). "And Abigail hasted, and arose, and rode upon an ass, with five damsels of hers that went after her; and she went after the messengers of David and became his wife."

David recognized the true virtue and beauty of Abigail. He, a king, did not waste any time after Nabal's death to make her his wife. Most would consider this quite shameful today. This was her reward, for a just woman regards her husband's life.

Strength and honor are her clothing, and she shall rejoice in time to come. Give her of the fruit of her hands, and let her own works praise her in the gates (Proverbs 31:25, 31).

She shall rejoice in eternity for her excellent works while she was young. Good works will reap good rewards (Revelation 2:23). The reference to the fruit of her hands validates that in the Bible, our hands are symbolic of our works. The virtuous woman takes great care that the fruit of her hands is worthy to be praised. As of Ruth 3:3, we learn that all the people of the city know that Ruth is a virtuous woman. In biblical times, everyone had to enter the city through the gates.

At the age of ten, I lived with my grandparents for a while. One day, we took a long ride; it turned out we were going to a funeral. My grandfather stayed with me outside until it was time to go in. We sat at the rear of the church. In my innocence, I blurted out, loud enough for the entire church to hear, "Who was she?" To which my grandfather replied, "She was a lady." "She must have been," I replied. "The church is full. I'll bet it isn't this full even on Sundays." Which would you like to be remembered for, being a lady or less than a lady? This woman's works did, indeed, praise her in this world as well as at the gates of heaven; I am sure. A woman who fears the Lord shall be praised just as this woman was (vs. 30b).

Another mark of a real lady is that she gives to the poor and needy. She stretches out her hand to the poor (vs. 20a). Her hand standing for her works indicates she will give a portion of her earnings to the needy. She will also minister to the needs of her husband. A virtuous woman is not overly occupied with having her needs met to the point where nothing or anyone else matters. "Charity suffereth long, and is kind; charity envieth not; charity vaunteth, not itself, is not puffed up" (1Corinthians 13:4).

As Matthew 25:34-40 says, feeding the homeless is equivalent to feeding Jesus Himself. Volunteer at a soup kitchen. Do it with the true spirit of serving Jesus as if He were sitting right there. This will bring real joy to your soul. It has for me.

NOTE: Under no circumstances should you to bring a homeless person into your home or let them know where your home is. An 18-year-old unwed mother in Boston allowed a homeless man to spend a night at her home. He violently beat her to death. Then there is the case of Elizabeth Smart who was kidnapped from her home and held for nine months by a homeless man. There are numerous shelters you can make donations to. If you choose to give directly to them, provide gift certificates from local fast food chains. This will prove difficult for them to convert to cash for other purposes.

"As we have therefore opportunity, let us do good unto all men, especially unto them who are of the household of faith" (Galatians 6:10). This opportunity only exists while we are alive and as long as we are alive. Verse 9 instructs us not to be weary in doing good for in due season; you will reap your rewards if you faint not. One sure way to lose heart is to expect or desire rewards from man. Sooner or later, you will be sorely disappointed if you do. What would be an example of doing good to others?

If a brother or sister is naked and destitute of daily food. 16 And one of you say unto them, depart in peace, be ye warmed and filled, notwithstanding ye give them not those things which are needful to the body (James 2:15).

Say not unto thy neighbor, Go, and come again, and tomorrow I will give; when thou hast it by thee (Proverbs 3:28).

Many times, I have heard people justify not giving to the homeless because they say they are just bums who do not want to work. Granted, some are, but some are not and truly are in need. Most do not collect enough to buy a meal each day. Include a tract or a small Bible with anything you give them.

HOW NOT TO BE A VIRTUOUS WOMAN

In this chapter, you will learn about the bumps in the road on the way to becoming a virtuous woman. If we recognize some of the subtle methods Satan uses to influence mankind, we will be better equipped to avoid them. Let's start by analyzing scriptures that relate to being a lady. Then, we will examine Satan's attempts to destroy these principles. With some examples and personal experiences, you will be better able to recognize when you are being led astray.

John 8:44 tells us that Satan is "a liar and the father of it" and "there is no truth in him." Having once typed, not written, an eight-page speech for the secular feminists, I can truthfully say their material is based on lies. God is the truth and the light, and He cannot lie (Titus 1:2). Following God's roadmap will lead you to the light of truth.

The heart of her husband doth safely trust in her, so that he shall have no need of spoil (Proverbs 31:11).

The heart is the part of ourselves with which we love, and which can be broken by infidelity (that is one type of "spoil"). The type of woman who has low morals is mentioned in Proverbs 12:4, "A virtuous woman is a crown to her husband: but she that maketh ashamed is as rottenness in his bones." What normal man would be proud of his wife's infidelity? On the contrary, infidelity is a cause for shame. "House and riches are the inheritance of fathers: and a prudent wife is from the LORD" (Proverbs 19:14).

Every wise woman buildeth her house: but the foolish plucketh it down with her hands (Proverbs 14:1).

I know of a woman who literally tore down her own house (at least the bathroom)! That is not what this verse is referring to. The "house," as used in this context is her marriage and family. Psalms 127:1 is another reference to the family as the house. In Scripture, our hands and feet are symbolic of our works and our ways, respectively (Proverbs 31:31). Here, God is talking about a woman ruining her marriage with her works, which can be done in many ways: 1) committing adultery and 2) playing games.

Games can include intentionally making her husband angry or jealous. The following two scriptures further support this: It is better to dwell in a corner of the housetop, than with a brawling woman in a wide house. It is better to dwell in the wilderness, than with a contentious and an angry woman (Proverbs 21:9, 19).

A brawling woman loves to stir up a fight and will undoubtedly destroy any happiness in her house. The German poet Heinrich Heine left his entire fortune to his wife, but with one catch, she had to remarry "Because then there will be at least one man to regret my death." "A continual dropping in a very rainy day and a contentious woman are alike" (Proverbs 27:15). No one likes either of these. King Solomon wrote Proverbs so it figures that he must have had, at least, one of these women in his harem. Women can remain in discord for hours; however, even if men's quarrels escalate into fist fights, they are usually finished afterwards, unless one of them is an absolute punk.

She will do him good and not evil all the days of her life (Proverbs 31:12).

A virtuous woman says only kind words to her husband. Don't meet him at the door when he comes home from work and unload all your days' dilemmas on him – wait until later. Words that have to be followed by "If you hit me, you will go to jail" are not kind at all; neither is nagging.

There should never be a time when a woman says this because of her husband. This brawling behavior refers to the way this type of woman talks to her husband, not how the husband addresses her. A virtuous woman's behavior is different. When she shares negative things, she does so with tact and diplomacy.

Both genders would do well to do as James 1:19 says. They should be slow to speak, swift to hear, and slow to wrath. "A soft answer turneth away wrath: but grievous words stir up anger. The tongue of the wise useth knowledge aright: but the mouth of fools poureth out foolishness" (Proverbs 15:1,2).

A virtuous woman does not merely look out for her interests. She will never be heard to say, "A girls got to protect her own interests." To be Christian means to be Christ-like. We did not give ourselves that name; the world coined it for us. Jesus died on the cross and made the ultimate sacrifice for us. He gave Himself unselfishly, with no thought whatsoever about what was in it for Him. Before He died, Jesus said, "Father forgive them," not "World, you owe me big time for this."

In the book, *A Return to Modesty* by Wendy Shalit[7], it is said: "In a sexual landscape without any rules, girls lacking male approval are more often taken advantage of, but today it is even thought to be sexist for a father to give away his daughter on her wedding day. That, we are told, is a concession to the view that women are property. Yet what is really so terrible about belonging to someone who loves you" Thinking that belonging to someone who loves you is terrible, is a twisted lie. Just as the woman belongs to her husband, the man also belongs to his wife.

A minister once said in a sermon "Love your children as you should, or they will go looking for that love somewhere else" (See I Timothy 5:8). Little girls without father figures will sometimes allow themselves to be sexually taken advantage of because they see sex as a way of acquiring the male approval they lacked as a child. I heard a grown woman admit this and her father was present in her life as a child. I had a visitor who told me he was working three jobs to provide his kids with presents and things. I suggested he take a day off to spend with his kids and see how they liked that as opposed to gifts.

Girls will also have sex to feel important to someone. However, they are on a slippery slope with no escape as long as they continue to seek the male presence they desire in this way. Homosexuals also target little boys who don't have the father figures they so desperately need. Females give sex to get affection, and some males will provide affection to get sex.

The biblical view of women as property is another lie the feminist quote to make malcontents of today's women. How else could Satan stir you up to help him overthrow so many of God's ordinances? He needs to do this to set up his anti-Christ. In truth, you are only liberating yourselves from the kingdom of God. Do not expect to inherit the kingdom of God if you are aiding and abetting Satan to become like God.

For a whore is a deep ditch, and a strange woman is a narrow pit. She also lieth in wait as for a prey and increaseth the transgressors among men. Thine eyes shall behold strange women, and thine heart shall utter perverse things (Proverbs 23:27-28; 33).

In this passage, "strange women" are women who seduce other women's husbands. "Thine heart shall utter perverse things" refers to what some men will think about when viewing this strange woman's flesh. The strange woman can use her body to ensnare men and deliver their souls to Satan. She is definitely a trap to men.

Always dress appropriately, not to tempt any man as I Timothy 2:9, 10 instructs godly women: "In like manner also, that women adorn themselves in modest apparel, with shamefacedness and sobriety; not with broided hair, or gold, or pearls, or costly array; (but which becomes women professing godliness) with good works." A woman must be diligent not to tempt men. Even unintentionally she can become a tool for Satan to use to bring men down; like the woman mentioned in this next verse.

Her feet go down to death; her steps take hold on hell (Proverbs 5:5).

Imagine a set of wind chimes. When the wind blows there is a sweet sound but once it stops there is nothing. A woman who has become a cheap imitation learns how to make sweet sounds but when sin shows through there is no longer any substance, just like the tinkling brass. Sooner or later, ugly sin will show through, and the real inner self will be exposed. It's always apparent when a woman has given up her virtue. Do not be deceived. Men can tell and so can women.

Women can deliberately or unintentionally tempt men with their dress and thereby become servants of Satan. Your husband is not included in this. But I say unto you, that whosoever looketh on a woman Mat 5:28 to lust after her hath committed adultery with her already in his heart. Just don't provide the images that would provoke men to lust.

Not tempting men does not mean you should gain a hundred pounds and let your teeth rot. Instead, it involves not exposing your physical charms to the whole world. It is perfectly all right to make yourself attractive, but it is not proper to dress seductively because of the psychology God gave to man. Men are sexually aroused by what they see. This explains why there are more female strippers than males. Attractive/seductive, whichever you chose defines what it means to be female to you.

Women peddling their flesh does not help other women in any way. If a woman uses her physical appearance to be noticed by men, she should not be surprised if that is all men want her for. If a female dresses to attract attention, she cannot pick and choose who looks at her. And she has to renounce some right to complain. After the physical attraction wears off, it will require something more to keep him interested. Never take that first step and then you will know if a man is interested in you, rather than something physical.

If you are a flirtatious woman, it should be no surprise if he has no respect for you either. When men have no love or respect for a woman, they will tell all. Loose lips sink ships. Have you ever heard a husband talk about the intimacies of his wife? Be certain, if you are in school and have sex, everybody will know. I asked a beautiful married woman who was seductively flirting with men, "Is that what it means to be a woman to you?" She ran away crying. Not when I asked her, "If your husband could see you, would he be happy with you?" and not when I told her God could see her also.

Sitting in church one Sunday, I looked around to see who was near me. I had to do a double take. One young girl sitting behind me had her charms out for the world to see. I certainly was surprised to see those in the church; hence the double take. However, she thought I was checking her out and went to complain to the pastor. I was summoned to the back of the church, which consisted of a half wall with glass that was open for the congregation to both see and hear us. The first thing I said was that it was just a double take because I was surprised. The second thing I said was that you could not pick and choose who looks at you when you dress like that. Then I asked her why she had bought and worn that type shirt. She said it was to attract the attention of the boys. Then I told her she was on a slippery slope destined to having sex. She claimed she would not and asked me what a slippery slope was. I told her a slippery slope is when you make one-step or move that will inevitably lead to another. By displaying her charms, she was making it increasingly difficult to avoid that destination.

I also told her once the interest in her charms wore off she would need to go one step further to retain the attention she had gotten and so on until she had sex. It ended with her crying in the bathroom, and she never wore that shirt again. Not three weeks later, she was complaining that one of the boys she had attracted wanted nothing more to do with her. She had learned the hard way that her body was all he was interested in. In biblical times, the prostitutes used to advertise their vocation by their attire. Prostitutes still do this today.

A television documentary on the life of Max Factor stated that until 1908, only prostitutes and actors wore makeup.[8] One of the first things the Feminist movement wanted to do was to wear makeup and smoke. There is a saying if it looks like a duck, walks like a duck, and quacks like a duck, it is probably a duck. Well, if it looks like a prostitute, you know the rest. I am sure at the turn of the century there was some confusion as to who were prostitutes or not when housewives started wearing makeup.

First Peter 3:3 talks about a woman's outward adornment also. There is nothing wrong with looking good or taking care of one's self, but you should not do it with the intention of tempting men. Look inward as well as outward because the true inner self will shine through. It speaks heaps about the type of man you want and will attract as well as the kind of woman you are.

My grandfather once showed me a photo taken of him when he was a teenager swimming with a group of his friends. The swimming suits were the usual type for the turn of the century, covering head to toe. In the center of this picture was a young girl about to jump off a small wooden bridge. My grandfather pointed out how her swimming suit stopped just below the knees. He said she had cut them off, for which she was arrested for indecent exposure. People from my grandfather's era would faint dead away if they went to a beach today.

In the mid-nineties, there was a significant debate on whether to keep the swimsuit competition in the Miss America beauty pageant. They had a picture of that year's winner and another of a contestant from the early 1920s in swimsuits. The woman from the `20s looked far more ladylike and elegant. I once went to a church picnic that had a private beach where we could swim. Some of the women's swimming suits left very little to the imagination.

Our bodies are the temples of God, and He said, "I will dwell in them, and walk in them" (2 Cor. 6:16). This is not what God wants women to do with his temple at all.

Whether a woman's swimsuit stops above or below the knees is irrelevant; if it arouses men, a real lady will not wear it. A real lady does not feel it is a burden to keep her body from tempting men. She realizes her body is not only hers; it is also God's temple. God neither made a woman to bring down a man nor a man to bring down a woman.

Know ye not that ye are the temple of God, and that the Spirit of God dwelleth in you. If any man defile the temple of God him shall God destroy; for the temple of God is holy, which temple ye are (1 Corinthians 3:16,17).

Defiling the body as mentioned in this verse, especially includes premarital sex for both sexes. It also applies to tattoos (Leviticus 19:28), illegal drugs, smoking, and drinking to excess. You have a covenant with God to keep His temple holy.

Beloved, believe not every spirit, but try the spirits whether they are of God: because many false prophets are gone out into the world (I John 4:1).

It is perilous to your soul not to test those you follow to ensure their words and teachings are not contrary to God's Word. If you blindly follow a group or organization (secular feminists) that propagates doctrines contrary to God's ordinances, you will fall into the pit along with those you follow (Romans 13:2).

For of this sort are they which creep into houses, and lead captive silly women laden with sins, led away with divers lusts (2 Timothy 3:6).

This sort that creeps into houses as discussed here were false teachers. Today, we call some of these false teacher's feminists. They easily lead silly women to follow them because these women cannot see the truth; if it were right in front of their faces. The word "divers" means that these women had more than one form of lust including greed, bearing false witness, and extortion.

Turn away from such teachers! I have seen marriages torn apart by the false leaders (feminists) of today and others that were shaken to their foundation. The first thing they will convince a new follower to do is to get rid of their husbands. Many foolishly do too. Henry David Thoreau made the famous statement: "Most men lead quiet lives of desperation, and go the grave with the song still in them." So, do many women. Most men go to work at just a job, so do most of the woman. You will not achieve any greatness following the worldly feminist and by destroying your marriage.

Satan has a movement going called feminists that lead silly women to try to liberate themselves from God's ordinances, but he cannot save them from hell. That is where he wants them, of course. For misery certainly loves company. Why would Christian women follow Satan? Hell is full of fools whom Satan has deceived. Satan is fully aware that he can never be like God. He will proclaim himself as God and mankind will worship him as such for a time. Except for a few tricks that he will be allowed to perform, he can never create anything as God has, and he knows that. So, his main method to become like God is to impersonate Him to intercept man's worship of the true God. For a time, he may be like God, but it will be a short deception upon man. Then he and his servants will be overthrown and cast into the bottomless pit. Rest assured that all who help him overthrow God's ordinances will be thrown into the pit with him, to eternal damnation and torment.

For Satan, to set himself up as God, he will have to overthrow as many of God's ordinances as he can. God has many truths besides the type this scripture refers to. It will not go well for those who turn any of his truths into lies. Follow truth, not lies, and you will be set free.

Who changed the truth of God into a lie, and worshipped and served the creature more than the Creator, who is blessed forever, Amen (Romans 1:25).

It is a true honor for a lady to retain all the virtues of her sex and being truly gracious will be a beginning to accomplish this. The word gracious means kind. Screaming and intentionally aggravating people are not kind deeds. As Proverbs 15:1 says, "A soft answer turneth away wrath: but grievous words stir up anger." It's been said, "Music tames the savage beast." That may or may not be true but if you ever meet a bear in the woods experts say not to yell and scream at it.

As said earlier, there is no need for a lady or anyone to scream unless someone is hurting her or there is a fire. Psychologists say that anger is the result of fear. This is hard to understand, but with some astute observation, it will become apparent to be true. Most people scream when they are angry. Ask yourself what do they have to hide because of their fear?

A gracious woman retaineth honor (Proverbs 11:16).

A virtuous woman will not manipulate or try to control her husband to gain the authority God gave to him (I Timothy 2:12). Doing these things will cause her to lose her husband's honor and respect among men. Marriage is merely a changing of command. What do you think the minister means when he asks, "Who gives this woman away?"

Nowhere in the Bible does God say, "Husbands, make your wives submit unto you." In Ephesians 5:22, God commands wives to submit to their husbands. God commanded women to do this for a reason. Perhaps, that is why the woman is called a helpmate in Genesis 2:20. The independence that the feminists teach is in direct conflict with this scripture. Where will this put them in God's kingdom or should I say hell? Even Jesus submitted to the cross so follow His example and submit to God's ordinances. He prayed saying, "Father, if thou be willing, remove this cup from me: nevertheless not my will, but thine, be done" (Luke 22:42). And again in Matthew 26:39 Jesus prays, "That if it be possible let this cup pass from me." Then He says in submission, "Not my will but yours."

While searching on the Internet for the Promise Keepers, I also found the feminists' rebuttal to them and their position on a wife's submission to her husband. The way the feminist attacked them if you did not know better, you would think that the Promise Keepers had written the Bible or, at least, this scripture.

I did not write the Bible either, but my part is in the telling also. Go to Matthew 5:19, 20 to learn where these teachers will end up and discover that you will go there with them if you throw your voice in with the feminists.

Reflect on your life for a moment, and you will likely remember a time when someone told you to do or not to do something without telling you the consequences of failing to heed their advice. It was probably a parent. Our Father in heaven is like that also. Often, the consequences of not obeying God's Scriptures are not readily apparent. I hope I have presented an idea of what can happen if you do not honor your husband.

Honoring your husband does not mean you are speechless. It means that if you disagree with him, you are to hold your tongue until you both are at an appropriate place and time to voice your disagreement. Perhaps, your home would be the correct place. Do this even if your husband is wrong. I've witnessed many Christian women jump on the side of other men when they were in arguments with their husbands. This is not only dishonorable to your husband but also does not look good if the other person you oppose your husband for is a man – especially if viewed by someone of the world. They know what it means when they do it. (I Timothy 5:22). This also applies to the husband who should give his wife the same respect. God is not one-sided.

The world gives strong recognition to the importance of the man as the head of the home. In the military, an officer's career can be adversely affected by his wife's actions if they are inappropriate. The reasoning behind this thinking is that a man who cannot keep his home in order cannot handle the authority and responsibility of rank, just as the minister mentioned below found out. Little surprise here considering I Timothy 2:5 says the same about a bishop.

I attended a friend's wedding some years ago. At the reception, I got to sit with the minister and his wife. Naturally, we started talking about the churches they were at while they were married. The minister's wife told me they spent about two years at each church. Naturally, being at a wedding, during the conversation she was telling me how tough it had been for them to stay together. This woman was quite vocal about her husband's faults. I told her that if she dishonored her husband, it would do nothing but diminish his parishioners' respect for him.

As she choked back tears, she asked, "It will?" She had just had an epiphany and realized she was the cause of her husband having to look for a new job constantly. Little did she understand the effect it would have on her life as well. For the two are one flesh. What affects one will unquestionably influence the other.

Habakkuk 2:15 says, "Woe unto him that giveth his neighbor drink, that puttest thy bottle to him, and makest him drunken also, that thou mayest look on their nakedness!" The nakedness mentioned here refers to a person's imperfections or the skeletons in his/her closet as we say today and also the person's fears. Without using a drink that is what the above minister's wife did to him by exposing his faults. He took her into his confidence and paid for it. This is an excellent example of the type of wife not to be. Never forget that you have your faults also; no one is without shortcomings. Real love will help us overlook the insignificant ones and help change those that are important. That's what for better or worse means. Always look for the better parts. For a happy marriage make sure the good times outweigh the bad by a ratio of 5 to 1.

"Too much alcohol will make you dance and drop your pants" (Quoted on television in the early 80's). I cannot add much to that. Too many women have ended up in bed with the wrong people as a result of consuming alcohol. Be careful that men do not put a strong drink in front of you to this end. You can be sure that if they offer you drugs, they want something in return because drugs are neither cheap nor good for you.

This is also a warning for young women and the men not to have a relationship with an alcoholic. A great deal of violence comes along with alcoholism. Be very cautious; Alcoholics are excellent at hiding their problems and courtship is a time of maximum deceit by both parties. There is a chance that an alcoholic male will be a child molester, particularly of his own children. A government study from The National Library of Medicine (Pubmed.gov) states Forty-nine percent of the child molesters were drinking at the time of the commission of the offense. The alcoholism rate for the group was 52% based on the MAST.

If all women decide to be ladies, then perhaps, the men will have no choice but to marry them. My experience has been that feminists teach if all women were alike (bad) then men would have to marry them. This just teaches women to take the easy way out. Being a lady is not the easy way. Women should realize that if they unite in the desire to be ladies, men would not have any choice in the type of women to seek. Despite what women have been told, men do not have to marry them if they are all worth less. A man's chances of having a long and happy marriage are better with a good woman.

Throughout history, the number of males to females has never been equal. Since males die more often than females eventually there are more females than males. 43 percent of all Americans over the age of 18 are single, according to the U.S. Census Bureau. For every 100 single women, there are only 88 unmarried men available. That comes out to be an awful lot of losers in the game of musical chairs called Life. So as Paul said, some are truly meant to be single. Since there are eventually more women than men, it would be wise to stack the deck in your favor and retain your virtue. If you were shopping for a dress and found one on the racks that were ripped and had holes in it, you would not buy it. Which woman will a gentleman want when he is interested in marriage? Given the surplus, he can be picky.

Here is a hint: most men are not going to marry a woman who has sex on the first date. The philosophy is, "If she does it with me this soon, she could do it with anybody." Studies have shown that sex is far more important to a smart woman.[9] In a magazine article, a woman was telling about one of her first dates and how he came with flowers, chocolates, and AIDS.

Favor is deceitful, and beauty is vain: but a woman that feareth the Lord, she shall be praised (Proverbs 31:30).

All individuals, male and female, have a point in their lives where they look their best, and after that, it's all downhill. Every day that you get up, you are one day closer to being on that downhill side. Do not put too much stock on how you or another person looks, for beauty is fleeting. In the words of a senior pastor, "Guys, you want the best-looking girl and girls, you want the best-looking guy. Look long and hard, for someday you will look over at them; and what is left of their hair will be white or gray. The wrinkles will be so deep they'll look like a prune. And as you look past them, you will see their teeth staring back at you from a glass. See how erotic that is".[10]

Beauty is deceitful if it makes you think it will make someone a good spouse. We have all seen people who believe they are just great because they're beautiful. Sadly, when their beauty is gone, so is their value. Beauty is nothing to be despised but do not be deceived into exploiting it. It is also very fleeting. I was in a friend's living room and noticed a picture of a bride in her wedding gown. I looked at the picture and then the woman of the house three times before I realized no one would have a picture of any other bride on her wall but the woman of the house. At that time, her oldest child was about 15 years old. The picture on the wall was that of a lovely bride. Needless to say, since it took three looks, she did not look the same.

In the days of the 45 records, there was this joke. Marriage is like a 45 record; you pick what you want on one side and take what you get on the other. If you choose a spouse for looks, sooner or later, you will end up on the flip side. Sometimes, it does not take long, but you will get there someday. Drinking and smoking will get you to the flip side sooner.

No matter how excellent a woman thinks she is, that will only get her so far and then she will become sickening to a man. Be very suspicious if another woman tells you that you are beautiful. Remember it is true that the feminists have openly embraced the lesbians. Why else would they fight for lesbian issues?

By the way, smoking and drinking are good ways to destroy beauty. Both introduce oxidants into the human body, which rob the skin of oxygen and destroy it. They affect the small blood vessels, called capillaries. I went with my sister to visit one of her friends who gave me a picture of a beautiful woman and said that it was her 3 years ago. She had changed so much I would not have known it was her had she not told me. Then she said her twin sister still looked like that. She cried when I looked at her and said: "She does not drink or smoke, does she?" As I said, there is nothing wrong with taking good care of yourself; just do not be deceived by physical appearances or use them to tempt men.

Think a great tan is necessary? Beware! The sun causes those brown spots we get when older. Hint: When and if you decide to have children, rub vitamin E cream on the areas likely to get stretch marks. If you already have them, do this daily during the pregnancy and afterward for a year. Internal ingestion of vitamin E pills will also help. Don't take more than 400 mg daily of vitamin E for extended periods. Studies have shown that it increases the chances of having a heart attack.

First Corinthians 15:33 says, "Be not deceived: evil communications corrupt good manners." Have you ever heard the expression, "Birds of a feather, flock together"? I have a cousin whose wife was associating with adulterers and eventually ended up talking just like them. Fortunately, she did as I advised and put away their company and filthy talk. This is the foolish talking that Ephesians 5:4 warns us all to avoid. Later, she learned that it was their sole ambition to commit adultery with her. The Devil is slow and patient to influence us in a deadly and subtle way. He has been at it for thousands of years, and he has the rest of our lives to work on us.

Put all such filthiness from your life. Do not be naïve; he has been working toward his goal of becoming like God ever since the day he crept into the garden.

When I was a freshman in high school, one of my female classmates was, as they say, the hottest girl in school. Even the teachers used to turn and look when she walked down the halls. Needless to say, all the boys wanted her, but she didn't allow anyone to touch her. She was a silver palace and a flawless ruby. She attended the Methodist church and was in the Brownies.

She always made the high honor roll. I moved and eventually graduated from a different high school. Several years later, I came back to our hometown and was sitting at the lunch counter at J. J. Newberry's. The woman who served me behind the counter was a dirty blonde with no shape to speak of and unattractive facial features. One of the other customers spoke to her by name, which was the same as the heartthrob of the school. In a small town, some things just never change. When she left, I took a chance and asked the patron who spoke if that was who I suspected she was. He replied that it was. Then he told me that she thought she used to be the hottest thing in school. I told him she was–I had gone to school with her. I asked him what happened to her good looks. He told me she got involved with two guys who influenced her to use drugs.

Then he lectured me on the hazards of drugs, and I told him I had never used them. At that time, I thought the authorities were stretching the truth when they told us drugs could ruin your looks, obviously not. A little later, I got to thinking that she was probably not making much more than minimum wage and decided to chance one more question. How could she afford drugs working here? The sad reply was that she was prostituting herself. Here was a young lady who used to have great looks, virtue, and intelligence but bad communications and company destroyed her. Much like Samson, she could have been a contender but never reached her full potential. We are not going to delve into the story of Samson and Delilah (Judge. 13-16) too much here, but I hope most of you are familiar with it so I won't have to. If not read Appendix B.

The Bible teaches us not to judge lest we are judged accordingly. However, you would be hard pressed to convince me that Delilah is in heaven. For how could someone who brought down a man of God like she did inherit the kingdom of heaven? Even if Samson had already fallen by his association with the wrong type of women, he still lost his strength because of Delilah's betrayal. Be not deceived: if you are married to a Christian man, and you dishonor and bring him down, you shall not escape. For God has said to honor your husband. Notice that nowhere did God say a husband had to deserve or earn his wife's honor. Marriages in most countries are no longer arranged as in the past; instead, couples marry for love. So, if you do not honor or respect a man in the first place, it is best not to marry him. We need to think with our heads as well as our hearts.[11]

In the following paragraph, I speak to you based on my opinion of things, not necessarily with any scriptural backing. This does not mean that what you are about to read is wrong. In biblical times, if members of royalty even appeared to be acting indiscreetly, they were taken out and had their heads chopped off (I Timothy 5:22). It is my opinion that as Christians, we are equal to royalty. I do not believe I am making any fallacy of equivocation in this comparison. As Christians, we are to inherit the kingdom of God because we are God's brides. In the end that is all that will remain.

The royalty of this world does not particularly impress me. Their conduct is not becoming that which is godly. Nowhere in the Bible does it say that having sex even a few times is OK before marriage. Ephesians 5:3 instructs us not to let fornication into our lives not once as becomes saints. Many women have been heard to say that if they could do it over again, they would have waited longer before they started having sex. It is a fact that once you start, it is very, very hard to stop, and every new partner is another flaw within you. It will not make a woman out of you either.

You cannot remove the mote from the eye of the opposite sex until you remove your own first. In other words, do not try to blame others if you succumb to temptation. I have heard many women lament the number of men who fool around on their wives. No matter how loudly they complain, they still cannot change the fact that they are the sex that these men are fooling around with. Women must take responsibility for their actions also. They must stop blaming the opposite sex for their faults and learn that it is their responsibility to say no. It is not right for a young man to ask for a virgin's virtue, but young girls must be taught that it is also their responsibility to say no. The fact that Eve handed Adam the forbidden fruit did not make his sin of eating it any less. He knew he was not supposed to.

GAMES

The Feminists teach that playing mind games will help you find out how committed a man is to you. This is not what you will find out at all. Remember where I stated I had typed a feminist speech. Do not be surprised if you find out he is not that interested, especially if you play games before your first date. The most likely scenario is you will attract the stalker type. I am not talking about the type of games you use to get noticed, like dropping your handkerchief as in olden times. What I am talking about is the kind of games where you have no respect for someone else's feelings. For example, trying to make him jealous of another guy, playing "hard to get" acting as if you're not interested in him or deliberately deflating his ego.

Jealousy games are dangerous games to play. If you are dealing with an insanely jealous type of man, you will deeply regret it – if you live too. At the very least, it will destroy his feelings for you.

Speaking of crushing a man's ego – that is what the feminists teach you to do when you want to get rid of a man and make sure he never comes back. They know that most men would rather be alone and unloved than rejected, ridiculed, and humiliated. Be sure that he will never come back, indeed, regardless if you ever change your mind. You also have an ego and would not like to have it bruised either.

Withholding sex is the ultimate rejection of your husband; that's why the worldly feminists teach you to have sex only when you want it, never when he does. I assure you; however, your relationship with your husband will never be complete if he has to keep his guard up from you to protect his true inner feeling and fears. Remember that true ladies and gentlemen never deliberately hurt others' feelings.

Before you play games like this, ask yourself, "Is this the level of equality I'm looking for? Would I like to be treated like that?" Have you been duped into thinking that you really are seeking equality? For if you were, you would have to answer, "Yes, I do want to be treated like that." This is a double-edged sword. No one likes to be toyed with, and the man will only put up with it long enough to fornicate with you. After he does (or when he realizes he never will), he will be gone.

I know of 50-year-old women who have not yet realized this. A lot of women who follow the feminists do not realize this until much later in their lives. Sooner or later, they will wake up. Sometimes, it is amazing how long it takes for a woman to connect to the fact that she gets dumped over and over again shortly after having the horizontal party.

I have known several beautiful women who played games for years, thinking that was the way to get a husband. The amazing thing is that after fifteen years, they had not awakened to the fact that it was not working. Married life is complicated enough; who wants to be married to someone who purposely makes it more difficult? Perhaps, these feminist games are one of the causes the divorce rate is so high.

One thing about games is that women do not play them, girls do. There are twenty-year-old women and fifty-year-old girls. Playing games is truthfully asking the question, "How much can I get away with?" Proverbs 31:12 says, "She will do him good and not evil all of her days." A virtuous woman does not play games. One of the problems with playing games is that once you find out how much you can get away with, you may have passed the point of no return. Add the difficulties created by game playing to those from normal married life and your marriage may not survive. You did not marry God. Unfortunately, your vows were not written in stone, and many couples seem to break them more often than not.

Whether you are a man or woman, playing such games reveals that you consider the other person nothing more than a toy. If someone respects you, they will not treat you like a toy. And if a person does not respect you, he or she is likely to cheat on you.

Finally, games are designed to bring the man down from the position God created for him. Feminist are indeed servants of Satan. Games also bring the woman down from her lofty position as well. No real man is going to submit to them because it belittles him. Sure, some men will, but once they have used you, they will be done with you. Using you was the only reason they put up with them. You are being manipulated so the hard-core feminist can disillusion you with men to turn you on to your own gender. No wonder if you are married and join them the first thing they say you will have to do is to get rid of your husband. Satan is attacking the family and destroying what it means to be a man and a woman.

GOD'S MERCY

If you have already lost your virtue, do not despair. It is never too late for God to give you a new spirit, for the old man died on the cross of Jesus.

And I will give them one heart, and I will put a new spirit within you; and I will take the stony heart out of their flesh, and will give them an heart of flesh (Ezekiel 11:19)

Unfortunately, you can never regain your lost virtue. You can still fulfill the remaining characteristics of the woman in Proverbs 31. A virtuous woman has many characteristics, which include being a woman of industry and godly character. The only woman referred to as a virtuous woman in the Bible is Ruth in the book of Ruth. Notice that she was a widow and also not a mother at this point in her life, but she still qualified as a virtuous woman. Ruth proves that the Proverbs 31 virtuous woman is not a fictitious character and being like her is possible to achieve.

God's mercy is infinite. John 8:3-11 tells of a woman taken in the act of adultery. In verse 11, Jesus tells her to go and sin no more. No matter how lost man gets, God will always be there to show the way home.

The Lord is not slack concerning his promise, as some men count slackness; but is longsuffering to us-ward, not willing that any should perish, but that all should come to repentance (2 Peter 3:9).

Recognize that repentance is unquestionably and unconditionally necessary for salvation. Second Samuel 7:22 and 1 Chronicles 17:20 both proclaim that there is none like God. They also say there is no other God. It is pretty difficult for insignificant mankind to do anything that God cannot forgive us for. God's mercy and love are always there for us, but we must seek them out. This is clear in the book of Matthew 12:31 and again in the book of Luke, "All manner of sin and blasphemy shall be forgiven unto men: but the blasphemy against the Holy Ghost shall not be forgiven unto men." Once God has forgiven you, do as Jesus said to the woman taken in adultery: "Go and sin no more."

Don't you find it difficult to forgive someone if they don't think they have done something wrong? A prime example of receiving forgiveness is seen in the account of the two thieves crucified with Jesus.

And one of the malefactors which were hanged railed on him, saying, if thou be Christ, save thyself and us. But the other answering rebuked him, saying, Dost not thou fear God, seeing thou art in the same condemnation? And we indeed justly; for we receive the due reward of our deeds: but this man hath done nothing amiss. And he said unto Jesus, Lord, remember me when thou comest into thy kingdom. And Jesus said unto him, Verily I say unto thee, today shalt thou be with me in paradise (Luke 23:39 – 43).

As we see in vs. 41, one thief admits his wrong, and in vs. 42 secures his salvation. However, the other is not included in Jesus' forgiveness. He neither sought it nor admitted that he was a sinner as the other thief did.

SOME THOUGHTS ON BEING A CHRISTIAN

One of the things being a Christian means is that there is more of a purpose to life than just to be born, live, and then to die. Life truly is a blessing from God. Get passionate about life! Look to Ecclesiastes 9:4-10 for more. Rejoice for time, and chance will happen to all (vs. 11). You are a light to the world, and you will have an opportunity to show that light. It helps if you have your heart set on the correct chances and opportunities. I know of some who have been converted to Christ simply by the example they saw in a Christian. I Peter 5:8 says, "Be sober, be vigilant; because your adversary the Devil, as a roaring lion, walketh about, seeking whom he may devour." On the other hand, some have been driven away from God by the example they saw in a Christian as well.

A college professor of mine once started class by discussing his lack of belief in God. I asked him if he had any proof and he shot back, "What proof of one do you have?" I said, "I have a book that was written thousands of years ago and is still a best seller. Plus, I have millions of fellow believers." I once attended a public speech by a scientist. I asked him so many questions; he wanted to know if I was a Christian. I told him I was, but that was not the reason for my questions. I told him I usually want to know how things work. I got him to confirm that scientists had determined that a person's soul weighs 27 ounces. I asked him how they had done that, but he did not know. Then I asked him what he thought happens after a person dies. He said that our souls go on living. Then I said, "So you do believe in life after death."

If you are a parent or when you become one, you will have a ministry because your life will influence your children. Your example will be their greatest teacher. But remember your adversary Satan will use every opportunity to make you fail. Nevertheless, always walk in righteousness. Sex is a very big weapon that Satan can use against you.

Being chosen for God's kingdom is an even more tremendous blessing. In Luke 10:22 Jesus said, "No man knoweth who the Son is, but the Father; and who the Father is, but the Son, and he to whom the Son will reveal Him." Second Peter 3:9 says, "The Lord is not willing that any should perish." Initially, God did not make hell for man, just for the fallen angels (Matthew 25:41). John 3:16 proves that God loves the whole world. He will tell all sinners to depart for he knows them not (Luke 13:27). That is tough love. To obtain salvation, we must confess that we are sinners. That does not mean to name our sins though like in the confession box at a Catholic church.

The first step to gaining salvation is to admit we are sinners. The real question is what do you want for your daughters? Do what I say not what I do? If this makes you uncomfortable think of this the next time, you get historical with your husband. "Correction is grievous unto him that forsaketh the way; and he that hateth reproof shall die" (Proverbs 15:10).

If we say that we have no sin, we deceive ourselves, and the truth is not in us. If we confess our sins, he is faithful and just to forgive us our sins, and to cleanse us from all unrighteousness. If we say that we have not sinned, we make him a liar, and his word is not in us (I John 1:8 – 10).

At the same time came the disciples unto Jesus, saying, who is the greatest in the kingdom of heaven? 2 And Jesus called a little child unto him, and set him in the midst of them, 3 And said, Verily I say unto you, except ye be converted, and become as little children, ye shall not enter into the kingdom of heaven. 4 Whosoever therefore shall humble himself as this little child, the same is greatest in the kingdom of heaven (Matthew 18: 1 – 4).

Once you have read this, it may be the only time you will be told about God. God is not willing that any should pass through this world without hearing of Him, at least, once. Get yourself to a church because this may be your one and only time you hear of Him.

God does not give us ordinances to consider but to obey. Come to the light of God because to love God is to obey Him. Far be it for me to judge who shall inherit the kingdom of God. But I fear for those who attempt to pull down so much as one of God's ordinances because they may not enter heaven (Romans 13:2).

Do not let these words stir up hate within you; they were written in the truth with the love of Galatians 6: 10. Come to love them as the light; whom the Lord loves He corrects. Write these words of wisdom on your heart; they are more precious than rubies and are a tree of life to those who lay hold on them (Proverbs 3:12-18).

In Daniel 9:23 the angel Gabriel tells Daniel he is greatly beloved. No wonder he survived a night in the lion's den. Daniel 10:12 gives us some insight as to why Daniel was loved so much by God, because he set his heart to understand and chasten himself before God. The Virgin Mary no doubt was also much loved to have been chosen to be the earthly mother of Jesus. Even God has His favorites whom He loves above all others. We know from John 3:16 that God loves the whole world. Both sexes, learn to open your hearts to understanding and chasten yourselves so you will also be greatly loved by not letting fornication and adultery be named among you even once as becomes saints (Ephesians 5:3).

Imagine if you will that this line represents' our walk-through life.

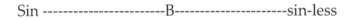

Sin ------------------------B----------------------sin-less

Let's define the ends of this line. They are never-ending so to the left represents more sin than is humanly possible for one person to commit. The right represents a state of being purely sinless, again, not humanly possible to obtain. The B represents where we are upon birth: neutral and sinless until we reach the age of accountability.

This line represents the fruit of our works. Even though we can never reach either end, we are all working towards one or the other. Living for God means that we are striving to reach as far right as we can. Even though we know, we will never reach it. Do not be confused; our works do not save us. Only by the grace of God as these two scriptures instruct us are we saved.

For by grace are ye saved through faith; and that not of yourselves: it is the gift of God: Not of works, lest any man should boast (Ephesians 2: 8-9).

Who hath saved us, and called us with an holy calling, not according to our works, but according to his own purpose and grace, which was given us in Christ Jesus before the world began (II Timothy 1: 9).

Know that Christ died for us so our sins may be forgiven (Roman 5:8). He freed us from sin, and our old man was crucified with Him (Romans 6:6). However, be certain that our works can still condemn us. We cannot continue in sin and expect to inherit of God's kingdom (Romans 6:1-5). The genuine fear of the Lord is to put off the old man and live by God's laws henceforth. Titus 2:12 validates this with instructions to live soberly in our present world. Denying worldly lusts is very important to our souls. Jesus says in Matthew 10:33 that whosoever denies Him before men, He will deny them before God.

The world will hate you if you truly deny worldly lusts for they will know you are not their own (John 15:18). Verse 14 proclaims that Jesus will purify and call to Him those who are zealous of good works. Likewise, he will not call those who are not desirous of good works.

For the grace of God that bringeth salvation hath appeared to all men, teaching us that, denying ungodliness and worldly lusts, we should live soberly, righteously, and godly, in this present world; Looking for that blessed hope, and the glorious appearing of the great God and our Savior Jesus Christ; Who gave himself for us, that he might redeem us from all iniquity, and purify unto himself a peculiar people, zealous of good works (Titus 2: 11-14).

Learn as Saul did in I Samuel 15:22 that it is better to obey God than sacrifice. Going to church on Sunday is important but what you do on Saturday night may well get your place in God's kingdom removed from you just as God removed Saul's kingdom from him.

It is time for an awakening and revival of God's church. Sadly, the church seems to be more and more influenced by the world. I heard a pastor lament that the world is changing the church, rather than the church changing the world. The church of today has not thrown off worldly lusts. Its young girls are only 14 percent more likely to be maidens on their wedding night than non-churched girls.[1] "Flee also youthful lusts: but follow righteousness, faith, charity, peace, with them that call on the Lord out of a pure heart" (2 Timothy 2:22). The church is also not immune from teenage pregnancy.

I heard a pastor on the radio proclaim, "Where Jesus is women are highly respected, but where he is not (Muslim/Taliban/Hindu), they are treated badly." Want to be treated respectfully? Go husband shopping at church.

God's righteousness is not for us to exalt ourselves with but to humble ourselves by recognizing and acknowledging that we are sinners (as the publican in Luke 18 does). The story of the publican explains the necessity of admitting we are sinners to receive salvation. Romans 2:11 demonstrates that God is no respecter of persons. He simply does not care who you are or whatever you may have done. He will not be standing at the gates when you arrive to greet you and tell you how lucky He is to have your presence – no not for even one of us. "Can a man be profitable unto God, as he that is wise may be profitable unto himself?" (Job 22:2).

In Luke 2:41-49, we read how Jesus stayed behind in Jerusalem as His parents left. After three days of searching, they found Him in the temple in the midst of the doctors, both hearing them, and asking them questions. When asked why He had stayed behind, He answered, "How is it that ye sought me? Wist ye not that I must be about my Father's business?" Matthew 6:9 instructs us to pray in this manner: "Our Father which art in heaven, hallowed be thy name." From this, we learn that we too call God our Father.

Jesus saith unto her, touch me not; for I am not yet ascended to my Father: but go to my brethren, and say unto them, I ascend unto my Father, and your Father; and to my God, and your God (John 20:17).

Rom 8:14 For as many as are led by the Spirit of God, they are the sons of God.

We can never be equal to Jesus in any way but learn from this that we too should be about our Father's business. Raising the children, He gives us to live godly lives is certainly one way to be about our Father's business. If we do not, we will answer for that when we stand before His throne. If we do, we shall lay-up treasures in heaven as these scriptures instruct us.

Lay not up for yourselves treasures upon earth, where moth and rust doth corrupt, and where thieves break through and steal: But lay up for yourselves treasures in heaven, where neither moth nor rust doth corrupt, and where thieves do not break through nor steal: For where your treasure is, there will your heart be also (Matthew 6:19-21).

He who dies with the most toys will never win. He can never take them with him, but those who have stored treasures in heaven will have them waiting. Matthew 10:42 tells us that we shall never lose our rewards.

There are only two choices: serve Satan or serve God. In the end, there will only be heaven and hell. "No servant can serve two masters: for either he will hate the one, and love the other; or else he will hold to the one, and despise the other. Ye cannot serve God and mammon" (Luke 16:13). Satan has many devices to turn us from God. Money is only one. Christians should focus on building riches in God's kingdom as well as fleeing from evil.

For the love of money is the root of all evil: which while some coveted after, they have erred from the faith, and pierced themselves through with many sorrows. 11 But thou, O man of God, flee these things; and follow after righteousness, godliness, faith, love, patience, meekness. 12 Fight the good fight of faith, lay hold on eternal life, whereunto thou art also called, and hast professed a good profession before many witnesses (1 Timothy 6:10).

Let them alone: they be blind leaders of the blind. And if the blind lead the blind, both shall fall into the ditch (Matthew 15:14).

In Matthew 15:14, Jesus is discussing the Pharisees with His disciples. In verse 13 of the said chapter, we see they were not of God when Jesus says that every plant not planted by God will be uprooted. Further, when Jesus told His disciples to leave the Pharisees alone, He knew there would be no turning them from their path to hell.

When he called them blind, He was referring to their knowledge of the real God, not being physically blind. Despite practicing religion, they were proud, ignorant and destined to hell. Those who followed them were also blind and would fall into the pit with them. Where does this leave the secular feminist and those who follow them?

It is not the intention of this material to reconcile the writings of James and Paul regarding our salvation. It is my unending desire to turn lost sinners from the error of their ways; thus, hiding a multitude of sins (James 5:20), specifically those who call themselves Christian and feminists. I wish it were possible to state this in a positive way, but sin in our lives has never done anything positive for us. God is ever merciful, and Jesus died for all our sins past, present, and the future. However, there are sins we commit that can cost us our salvation such as the sin of apostasy mentioned by Hebrews 10:26: "For if we sin willfully after that, we have received the knowledge of the truth, there remaineth no more sacrifice for sins." This sin occurs when men despise and reject Christ and His salvation or abandon their faith.

Learn that God is patient, and He will leave room for a lost sinner to repent as He did for Asa in 2 Chronicles 16:8-13. I truly fear that a Christian woman who joins the secular feminist movement is committing that sin, and I write that she may repent before her soul is lost.

Romans 1:25 speaks of those who have changed the truth of God into a lie. This scripture refers to homosexuality. How will it apply to you if you call yourself a Christian and a feminist? Well, consider this: the other feminist movement has openly embraced the lesbians. No one can turn God's truth into lies and escape. As

I have stated elsewhere, I have typed up a speech for the secular feminist movement, and I can personally guarantee you they deliberately build their doctrine on lies. We know the father of all lies and all those who do his lying will be with him in hell.

Out of the abundance of the heart, the mouth speaks (Matthew 12:34). For every idle word that man speaks they shall be accountable for (vs. 36). By those words, you shall be justified and condemned with them also (vs. 37). If you denounce God's truth, you are not following God and will face His judgment. Our works can condemn us nevertheless, James 2:20 says that faith without works is dead. Do you not know that the dead shall be judged according to their works? (Revelation 20:12). God will give everyone according to his or her works (Revelation 2:23).

We may not lose our places in heaven, but we can still bring ourselves down to be called the least in heaven (Matthew 5:19). However, (vs. 20) warns that our righteousness must exceed that of the scribes and Pharisees; otherwise, under no circumstances will we enter heaven. Just as there are different degrees of punishment in hell, there are different rewards in heaven (Deuteronomy 32:22 and Matthew 5:19).

Let's consider Romans 13:1 and 2: "Let every soul be subject unto the higher powers. For there is no power but of God: the powers that be are ordained of God. Whosoever, therefore, resisteth the power resisteth the ordinance of God: and they that resist shall receive to themselves damnation." Verse 1 refers to the governments and that as Christians, we should obey them because they are not in existence without God's consent (see Titus 3:1).

He will bring them down when He chooses as He did with King Saul, not us. God forbid that I should add to or say that God's scriptures mean something they don't.

No matter how I read verse 2, I cannot see where it separates resisting the power of man's rule from resisting any of God's ordinances. It seems like God just made it an ordinance of His to obey man's powers. To me, it equates opposing man's powers as being equal to resisting God's laws then the sentence of damnation is foretold. Look up damnation in a Bible dictionary, and you will see it means condemnation. It's not wise to resist God's ordinances unless you can find a scripture stating it's OK. Which I am sure you will not.

It is logical to believe from these two verses that you will bring condemnation to your soul. Isaiah 55:9 instructs us that God's thoughts are higher than ours. Have no doubt that God's ordinances are higher than man's, which unquestionably lead to condemnation for resisting them as well as mans.

So, what exactly is the difference between resisting and breaking God's ordinances? Let's start out by using Ephesians 5:22 as an example: "Wives, submit yourselves unto your own husbands, as unto the Lord." Apparently, breaking this ordinance is simply the act of a woman refusing to submit to her husband. The independence the feminists teach leads many women to violate this ordinance and thus, is a shining example of those who resist the power of God.

This became evident to me one day in church when the teacher read Ephesians 5:22 and a Christian woman who considered herself a feminist said, "They have twisted that all around." Now, this woman had managed to keep herself liberated from marriage so it was impossible for her to break this ordinance but clearly what she did was an act of resistance. As Christians, we should remember Matthew 12:36, "That every idle word that men shall speak, they shall give account thereof in the day of judgment."

The following two scriptures are the ones you need to be concerned about the most if you call yourself a Christian and a worldly feminist. The scribes and Pharisees of that day are here condemned for their outward appearances of religion but inwardly were not holy. Here we learned that there are great and small commandments; whosoever tries to weaken the importance, and our obligation to obey even the least of them will bring peril to their souls. Like the scribes and Pharisees did for teaching others to do as they did. Ask yourself if those called the "least in the kingdom" are even in the kingdom. Meaning, are the least being referred to here as those in hell? As you read this book, seek to find out where the worldly feminists oppose God's ordinances.

Whosoever therefore shall break one of these least commandments, and shall teach men so, he shall be called the least in the kingdom of heaven: but whosoever shall do and teach them, the same shall be called great in the kingdom of heaven. For I say unto you, that except your righteousness shall exceed the righteousness of the scribes and Pharisees, ye shall in no case enter into the kingdom of heaven (Matthew 5:19,20).

Misery does love company, and Satan wants all the company he can get. When it says "In no case enter into heaven" that means no tears, or pleading will get you in.

85

"What doth it profit, my brethren, though a man say he hath faith, and have not works? Can faith save him?" (James 2: 14). "The demons also fear and tremble to no avail" (James 2:19). The belief of the demons will not save them because they have rejected God and joined Satan to overthrow Him. By the way, I have skipped ahead to the ending – and they lose – as will all who join Satan in turning God's truths into Satan's lies. If you are a Christian and a worldly feminist, ask yourself if you are telling God's truth or Satan's lies. Merely professing with one's mouth that you believe in God will not gain salvation. Our works must be based on obedience to the gospel.

What then? shall we sin, because we are not under the law, but under grace? God forbid (Romans 6: 15).

Write these words on your heart and love them as the light; for they were written for you in God's love. Keep as much sin as possible from your life, and God will reward all you do abundantly.

For then shall be great tribulation, such as was not since the beginning of the world to this time, no, nor ever shall be. And except those days should be shortened, there should no flesh be saved: but for the elect's sake those days shall be shortened (Matthew 24:21-22).

In the above verse, we see that Satan's subtle lies are so seductive even God's most elect may be deceived if allowed to be subject to them indefinitely. With sex, homosexuality and the violence depicted on television today, you must be ever vigilant in your children's lives as well as your own. That goes for the female homosexuals also known as feminists as well.

King Solomon was the smartest man who ever lived or ever will (I Kings 3:12). Scientists have estimated Solomon's IQ at 300. The average person's IQ is about 100. A genius has an IQ of, at least, 140. Yet, the smartest man who ever existed let his heart be turned away from God by his many foreign and forbidden wives. When he was old, he set up high places unto his wives' false gods. And God told him for doing that, "I will rend the kingdom from thee." Those of the Light should, indeed, have nothing to do with darkness. Solomon's constant exposure to Satan's wiles through his wives brought him down.

Lastly, I would like to apologize to 75% of those who may be converted to Christianity by this material. You see, it is a sad fact that Christians have the same success rate as heroin addicts. Within five years of going through a drug program, 75% of them will end up the same way they were when they started. Why apologize for saying that? Look at II Peter Chapter 2 to understand. And Jesus said unto him, "No man, having put his hand to the plough, and looking back, is fit for the kingdom of God" (Luke 9:62).

For if after they have escaped the pollutions of the world through the knowledge of the Lord and Savior Jesus Christ, they are again entangled therein, and overcome, the latter end is worse with them than the beginning. 21 For it had been better for them not to have known the way of righteousness, than, after they have known it, to turn from the holy commandment delivered unto them. 22 But it is happened unto them according to the true proverb, the dog is turned to his own vomit again; and the sow that was washed to her wallowing in the mire (II Peter 2:20 – 22).

In verse 20, escaping the pollution of the world means to be converted or called out of the world by obtaining a personal relationship with our Lord and Savior Jesus Christ. After conversion, if the people return to the lust of the world and become re-entangled, they are worse off than they were before being converted. As a matter of fact, verse 21 suggests they are now going to be worse off than if they had never been converted. The reference to the lowest hell in Deuteronomy 32:22 proves that there are different degrees of punishment in hell.

Proverbs 18:24 tells us: "A man that hath friends must shew himself friendly: and there is a friend that sticketh closer than a brother." This friend who sticks closer than a brother is Jesus. When man fails you, He will not. Trust me; man will fail and disappoint you but what a friend we have in Jesus.

I will not go into too much debate as there seem to be many different opinions on this. However, I personally believe that the reestablishment of Israel starts the clock for Jesus' second coming. I firmly believe we are in the last days.

This know also, that in the last days perilous times shall come. 2 For men shall be lovers of their own selves, covetous, boasters, proud, blasphemers, disobedient to parents, unthankful, unholy, 3 Without natural affection, trucebreakers, false accusers, incontinent, fierce, despisers of those that are good, 4 Traitors, heady, high-minded, lovers of pleasures more than lovers of God; 5 Having a form of godliness, but denying the power thereof: from such turn away. 6 For of this sort are they which creep into houses, and lead captive silly women laden with sins, led away with divers lusts, 7 Ever learning, and never able to come to the knowledge of the truth (II Timothy 3:1-7).

These days, we are seeking more knowledge than ever before in history. We send probes deep into outer space. There have been phenomenal advances in medicine. However, we still die. Yet, there are still seven thousand diseases without a cure. Yes, man is working on extending our lifespans. But we will never be able to learn the truth without God. I was talking to my niece, and I told her without God she is nothing. Learn to think for yourself. Only then will you escape the label "silly woman." Today is the information age where we need to learn all that we can. Just do not think you know so much that you can live without God as so many believe.

"Whoso loveth instruction loveth knowledge: but he that hateth reproof is brutish" (Proverbs 12:1). Needless to say, since this is my third edition, I have heard the question: "How can a man teach a woman how to be virtuous." The answer will cause someone some pain, but growing is about learning. I have shared this with several women, but they never came back. But that will not stop me from sharing the truth.

Whatever God's calls you to do – do it. Jonah ran but did not escape from God. What women think about a man telling them how to be godly women will not stop me from answering my calling. That is my part in this; it is up to you what you do with your new-found truths. I recently shared the meaning of Song of Solomon 8:8 – 9 to a woman and she went into the next room and cried because she wished someone had told her that when she was younger. Who is going to stop me? The feminist's I think not.

Nightmares are vividly realistic, disturbing dreams that wake you from a deep sleep. They often set your heart pounding with fear. Nightmares tend to occur most often during rapid eye movement (REM) sleep when most dreaming occurs. One night, in my sleep, I rolled onto my tape recorder and heard the voice of one of my female college professors in bed with me. That is the stuff nightmares are made of. Well, another night after reading Ecclesiastes 9:10, I had a dream in which everything was black. I could not speak or think. It was very difficult to escape from. I remember this because as I have mentioned in most nightmares except this one something horrible is usually chasing you. Yes, indeed work for God with all your might while you yet live. Nothing else will last.

Whatsoever thy hand findeth to do, do it with thy might; for there is no work, nor device, nor knowledge, nor wisdom, in the grave, whither thou goest (Ecclesiastes 9:10).

DATING

Now that arranged marriages are a thing of the past, in this day and age, most will date their spouses before marriage. More than 50% of all first marriages fail, as do 50% of second marriages. It comes as no surprise that 50% of all engagements are broken as well. You will not find the right person wasting your time with the wrong one. If after three years or so and your partner still has no idea if your relationship will lead to marriage, he or she never will.

At what age should parents allow their daughters to date? Some parents suggest eighteen. I consider sixteen to be a good age also, as do the authors of *Why Wait*. Any time before that, they are just too immature to handle it properly. It also gives you a chance to be involved as opposed to waiting until they are out on their own – say in college. Letting them date before the age of sixteen is like throwing them to the wolves. Believe me; the wolves know they are coming and how to spot them.

During my senior year in high school, two sisters were not allowed to date until they were eighteen. One of them ended up pregnant, and the other had sex on her first date. This is being offered as food for thought because it is a matter of upbringing and not so much a case of sheltering them; these sisters were not raised in a religious home. Of course, in a Christian house, protecting your children may still be necessary as discussed in the chapter titled "Silver Palace."

It would be wise to consider a child incapable of handling a relationship. The number of divorces today proves that a lot of adults cannot either. Do not expect a child to be able to handle situations that adults cannot. The types of people they choose to befriend early in life are going to be the same types they gravitate to for the rest of their lives. This is the reason you want to be involved in their dating choices. We are drawn to familiar things and people whether they are good for us or not. This is called Repetitive Compulsion; we do it because we think next time, we will get it right.

In college, I joined the equestrian club. There were all age groups at the lessons, and one night, I got into a conversation with a 13-year old girl about her dating choices. She flippantly told me it was none of my business. I replied it was a good thing it was not because if it were, she would not be able to date or have a boyfriend until age 16. I pointed out that she had not made any good choices and clearly was not capable of handling relationships yet. Her first boyfriend put her down and threatened to beat her up if she dumped him. I had to tell her she was a loser if she put up with that to get her to end that relationship. Later, I heard her complaining that her second boyfriend was putting her down also. After a heated conversation with her mother, she decided she was not going to let her have any more dates or boyfriends until she was 16.

If, while in school, your daughter is asked out by a much older boy, you should ask her to think about whether he feels that she is just easy pickings because she is much younger than him. Tell her not to date the older boys until she is a grown woman because they are not interested in marriage yet. Only when they are both adults will she be equal to him in his eyes. Make your children a part of the decision, rather than just telling them. My niece was barely 16, and the guy was 20. She was oh, so impressed and became an unwed mother. Do not let your daughters date the older boys; it is a recipe for trouble.

If any male tries to make you feel obligated to him after a date, do not go out with him again. He is no gentleman, and the rules of a gentleman's conduct do not apply to him. It could prove very dangerous for you to do so. Also, never accept a ride from him until you are confident he is a perfect gentleman. This means you will have to take a taxi. Do not worry about the cost; if you are living right, this is an investment in your future. Otherwise, you are only out for what you can get, which makes your actions no more righteous than his.

Not everyone who asks you out is necessarily head over heels in love with you but may just want to see if anything could develop. So, take a chance and go out if the person seems decent. If you know there could never be any interest, then politely explain and decline. True ladies and gentlemen never deliberately hurt anyone's feelings. You could say, "I do not want to hurt your feelings, but I am just not interested. Asking again will not change that." Do not think they will still be interested months or years later either.

Remember how I said to watch how someone treats other people because that is how they will treat you eventually? Well, someone may be watching you, especially if you like to embarrass people or hurt their feelings when they ask you out. Someday, you may be interested in someone but if he has observed your rude or cruel behavior, he may not want the same treatment from you and will never ask you out.

Proverbs 11:16 confirms this when it says that a gracious woman retains honor. On the flip side, a cruel woman will lose honor and respect.

I have some information to share that, if followed, will help ensure that more first marriages succeed. Having read a book titled *Dating in the 90's*, I remember the author imploring people if they broke off an engagement, to never go back to that person. He never stated why but repeatedly emphasized the need never to look back. Naturally, this made me curious as to why. Being a member of a group called Parents Without Partners (PWP), I had the opportunity to survey a group of the members. At a meeting with sixty or more people in the room, I verified with a show of hands that everyone there had been divorced. Then I asked if there was anyone who could say that he or she had not broken up with an ex, at least, once before marriage. Not one person in that room raised a hand. I could not raise my hand either.

So, the moral of this is, whenever an engagement is broken, do not go back to the person. The statistics are all against you. The decision to break up was made long before it actually happened. I would further like to recommend that you follow the advice of one of my eighth-grade teachers: "If your future spouse's relatives like you enough to tell you not to marry the person, do not do it." I sorely wish I had followed this advice.

I have it from a very reliable source that in the Air Force if one of their missiles ever becomes engulfed in flames, their orders are to "Run Hard" as a course of action. So, if you ever break an engagement or a relationship, "Run Hard." Do not look back like Lot's wife did.

It never ceases to amaze me when many men seek to disprove God's words. Yet, very often, many studies conducted by men simply prove God's words. God's truths are still His regardless if worldly men discover them on their own. A preliminary study I found in a magazine concluded that people who are honest are less likely to cheat on their spouses. No big surprise because Luke 16:10 says "He that is faithful in that which is least is faithful also in much: and he that is unjust in the least is unjust also in much." Look at a person's honesty very closely when dating them.

Courtship is a time of maximum deceit on both party's parts. Watching how the person you date treats other people is an excellent indication of how he/she will eventually treat you. Especially, keep an eye on how the person treats his/her parents. If the person mistreats his parents, regardless of how much he denies it, he will treat you the same.

There was once a couple who lived together for fifteen years, got married and a year later got divorced. How is that for deceit? According to research done by the Ohio State University, a history of cohabitation hints at a lack of commitment, an ability to end a serious relationship, and knowledge that there are other options out there besides this marriage. A marriage is more likely to last if neither you nor your wife used to live with another partner. If one of you did, your chances of divorce skyrocket 209 percent.

Some signs that you are dating an abusive person are jealousy, controlling behavior, isolating behavior, hypersensitivity, frequent mood changes, blaming others, and verbal abuse. It's true that opposites attract, don't assume that the qualities you fell in love with are going to keep a marriage together.

According to a study published in American Sociological Review, the biggest factor leading to divorce is the husband's job status. Harvard researcher Alexandra Killewald crunched the numbers and found that men who didn't have jobs or who had been out of work for a long time had a statistically higher chance of getting divorced in any given year, compared to those with stable careers. Per Killewald's study, men without jobs increase their odds of divorce by roughly 30%. What you really need to know is that there was a clear correlation between employment status and divorce rates.

(From 6 Signs Your Partner Is Good Marriage Material from Terry Gaspard, MSW, LICSW who also manages *http://movingpastdivorce.com/*)

Who we choose to marry is one of the most important and costliest decisions a person will make; yet, it's not uncommon for lovers to make errors in judgment. Why does this happen? One reason is that most of us aren't raised with healthy templates of marriage to follow. We also lack self-awareness and may be afraid of ending up alone.

Another factor is unrealistic expectations of marriage because we grew up in the first generation for whom divorce continues to be accepted and common. According to author Pamela Paul, lots of marriages seem to be trial marriages and people tie the knot with the notion of, "If it doesn't make me happy, I'll just move on." Since more and more individuals grow up in divorced homes where they witness divorce being the solution to marital problems, they may not approach marriage with a thoughtful mindset.

5 Questions to Ask Potential Marital Partners

1. **Who are your parents?** Include questions about marital history, mental illness, and substance abuse, etc. Don't shy away from asking questions now that may blindside you later. It's

better to be forewarned because some qualities have genetic components.

2. **What is your typical way of dealing with conflict?** Don't assume that your partner has good anger management skills. Does he/she usually take responsibility for his/her actions or blame someone else? Does he/she tend to stonewall or withdraw from conflict or see it as an opportunity for growth?

3. **How do you feel about having children?** How many children does he/she consider the best number if the person wants them? Does the person believe couples should share chores and childcare responsibilities?

4. **What are your values and beliefs about infidelity?**

5. **What is your view of divorce?** What would he/she consider an excellent solution to a period when your marriage is rocky?

There is no such thing as a perfect partner. You might want to ask yourself this question: Is there something about the way he/she treats me that makes me a bigger and better person? If the answer is no, ask yourself: Am I settling for less than I deserve in the relationship? *It seems a lot of people do settle for less as 70% of married people would trade up.*

And the Six signs are.

1. You admire your partner for who he/she is as a person. You like and respect who he/she is and the way the person carries him/herself through the world. If you can't respect a person's lifestyle, let alone admire them as an individual, it's hard to keep any relationship going.

2. Your partner is trustworthy because he/she keeps agreements. The person's actions and words are consistent. When you share something personal, you trust your partner will keep it confidential.

3. He/she makes time for you on a regular basis. The person makes you a priority because he/she values your relationship. Even when your partner is swamped, he/she makes time to spend with you.

4. Your partner is comfortable talking about the things that interest you and asks you questions about your hobbies, friends, and family. He/she appreciates you for who you are right now and the person isn't trying to change you.

5. He/she makes you feel good about yourself. A partner who genuinely cares about you is a boost to your self-esteem. He/she values you and gives you compliments and praise.

6. You share a vision. Sharing a dream for your life together can help you gain a healthy perspective. When couples possess a shared vision, the inevitable ups and downs of marriage are less bothersome. Creating a larger context of meaning in life can help couples avoid focusing on the small stuff that happens and to keep their eyes on the big picture.

If you feel your partner is the right person for you, but you still fear commitment, you might want to consider the following:

- Understand that no relationship is conflict-free, but you are worthy of having a relationship that makes you happy. If you aren't there yet, embrace where you are now.

- What is it that holds you back from achieving a satisfying relationship? And once you have it, what will you do when you get there?

The best partner will compliment you and bring out your very best. When you are with him or her, you will begin to see untapped possibilities within yourself and in the world. In any relationship, you will face ups and downs and your love will be tested. However, where admiration and respect are found, love will be sustained. But where these things are absent, love will die. Finding a partner who likes and respects you as much as you do him/her will give you the best chance of finding long- lasting love.

MARRIAGE

Be ye not unequally yoked together with unbelievers: for what fellowship hath righteousness with unrighteousness: and what communion hath light with darkness? (II Corinthians 6:14).

The above verse not only applies to marriage but other things in our lives. Never go into business with a non-believer. If you are a Christian and marry a nonbeliever, do not be surprised if they think like the world in that "It's just sex." For unbelievers will not have a sense of the loss of their souls as Christians should if they commit adultery. Where Jesus is, women are highly regarded; they are not viewed with the same regard and respect by the Taliban, Hindus or any other religion. You will not be either if you are married to a non-believer.

Be not unequally yoked in other things as well as religious beliefs. Being unequal in other things like intelligence and race will bring discord to your marriage. This does not mean such marriages cannot survive; it's just that there is additional baggage coming along with your partner. As I Corinthians 7:28 says, married people will have trouble in the flesh. A day will come when you will regret getting married. This applies to everyone, male or female, no matter who you married.

Proverbs 15:27 is another example of how a marriage can be turned into misery. It states: "He that is greedy of gain troubleth his own house; but he that hateth gifts shall live." Greedy people are just plain miserable to live with – male or female. No doubt since Jesus' love is about what he could give us and not get. You cannot love one another when your sole ambition is towards yourself. Those who are in love with themselves have very little competition. Is marriage to a worldly feminist who says, "A girls got to protect her own interests" going to be a good one? Not very likely. "So are the ways of every one that is greedy of gain; which taketh away the life of the owners thereof" (Proverbs 1:19). And anyone married to them as well.

Learn to ride out the storms in life. Researchers studying marriage at the University of Washington say, "Successful couples balance out any negative interactions with positive feelings and actions like showing interest, being affectionate, showing they care, being appreciative, smiling, paying compliments, laughing or showing concern." Remember marriage is a covenant with God that must be honored.

As a woman, if you were converted after getting married and are now joined with a non-believer, you are instructed in I Peter 3:1 to be in submission to your husband regardless if he believes or not. You do so that he may be won over by your conversation and by the example of your behavior.

When God provides us with a mate, he or she is much more than a warm body. Genesis 2:24 says that the husband is one flesh with his wife, so he is to be his wife's provider and protector. Imagine where we would be if men united like the feminists and refused to fulfill this commandment from God.

Ephesians 5:25 tells husbands to love their wives even as Christ loved the church and gave Himself for it. This means that Jesus died for His bride, the church and that a man should be willing to die for his bride as well. Therefore, married men are more willing to die – and I thought it was the henpecking. That is a lot to ask. Should a man be willing to do this for less than a godly woman? (See also I John 15:13). Are you dating someone you don't feel is worthy, then stop. Ephesians 5: 22-24 commands wives to submit to their husbands, not men in general. This submission neither makes her inferior nor does it mean husbands are to be tyrants.

Instead, it means that wives are to accept their husbands as the heads of their homes. They will not try to gain his authority as such. This submission is the wife's service to the Lord. A relationship of love/submission makes for a beautiful marriage; it is a great blessing for living a godly life for both.

Titus 2:4 instructs the older women to teach the younger women to be sober, to love their husbands and their children, to be self-controlled, pure, kind and lastly, obedient to their own husbands. This will earn young wives and mothers the respect of others and prevent God's Word from being maligned. Why older women and not younger ones? Perhaps, they have experience. How do you get experience? By making mistakes. This is a perfect example of learning from other people's mistakes because you will not live long enough to make them all yourself.

Notice here that you have to be taught how to love your husband. It is not acquired but must be learned. Some men have to be taught how to love their wives as well. Go to the "Guys Only" chapter for some helpful hints that will make your marriage happier for both of you. If any woman advises you to "play games," you should think long and hard on this. An unmarried woman is not likely to have any good advice on how to catch or keep a husband. Neither will a man-hating feminist.

If their methods of attracting a husband have not worked for them, what makes you think it will work for you? Be careful of whose advice and instructions you follow.

The gift of love is a precious one that is being eroded and destroyed by Satan's servants the secular feminists. They teach the love of self – what you can get for being a woman. Having someone to love and who loves you is a blessing from God that should be valued. You see, God's love has always been proven by what He does for us. Remember we were made in His image and the ultimate expression of His influence on us is our love for our fellowmen, with our spouses being held above all others (See I John 13:34).

The more sin there is in the world, the more God will distance himself from man. "But your iniquities have separated between you and your God, and your sins have hid his face from you, that he will not hear" (Isaiah 59:2). Remember the great flood? In Genesis Chapter 6, "The earth also was corrupt before God, and the earth was filled with violence. And God looked upon the earth, and behold, it was corrupt, for all flesh had corrupted his way upon the earth. And God said unto Noah, the end of all flesh is come before me; for the earth is filled with violence through them, and behold, I will destroy them with the earth" (vs. 11-13). "But Noah found grace in the eyes of the Lord. These are the generations of Noah: Noah was a just man and perfect in his generations, and Noah walked with God" (vs. 8-9).

Talk about being able to resist peer pressure! All flesh had corrupted itself, but Noah was a just man. It was the original sin that got mankind cast out of the garden. Sin distances God from man. God's love never varies (James 1:17). In Genesis 3:8, God walked in the garden amongst man but never again since the original sin. The more sin enters a marriage, the less love there will be. Loving only oneself is sinful (II Timothy 3:2). No one can continually give love without receiving love in return, not even God. Feminists have ruined many marriages with their love of self-ideology. The very word *agape* means love for others. "Beloved, let us love one another: for love is of God, and every one that loveth is born of God and knoweth God. He that loveth not knoweth not God; for God is love" (I John 4:7-8). Loving only oneself can only bring misery and destruction into a marriage. Those who are in love with themselves have very little competition.

To be Christ-like means to be like Him, to give to others without requiring or expecting something in return. Very little in the Bible focuses on what we should get but what we should be. Then we find out what we should get for this, such as the meek shall inherit the earth. This does not mean we should lose our lives for others, but those who do shall find life eternal. Hence, we should have agape love towards others. Even more, love should go to our spouses. This should be true for both partners. Marriage does not go well when either spouse is solely interested in what she or he can get. In the latter times, mankind shall be lovers of themselves.

The current divorce rate certainly reflects that (2 Timothy 3:2) When the Bible talks about the hereafter, it does not mean the same thing it says in the phrase, "What am I here after?" Let us compare love to a beautiful flower. To keep it healthy and alive you need to water and trim it regularly. To keep love alive, you must continuously nurture and care for it. Never act like a child and use it as a license to get away with behaving as badly as you want to. Even though marriage is to be for a lifetime, it is not written in stone, unless you are married to God, which you are not. Jesus commands in Matthew 19:9 that no one can put away

104

his/her mate except for fornication. Moses granted divorces because of the hardness of man's heart. You can diminish or destroy your mate's love because mankind's love is ever varying unlike God's. Even the church suffers the same percentage of divorces as the world does today.

If you can say you would not have treated your spouse the way you do now before you married him or her, then you need to pay particular heed to this warning about how you should treat your spouse. Mankind is ever changing and is not a rock like God. This is a wake-up call for those of you who think you can leave your spouse and then come back later whenever you are ready. Yes, I have seen people do this.

Love is not like a water hose; once you turn it off, you cannot turn it back on again. For those who sin willfully, there is indeed no more sacrifice for sinning (Hebrews 10:26). This scripture is referring to those who abandon their faith in God; they will no longer have a sacrifice. It goes without saying that those who will leave or destroy their marriages may not have any sacrifice that will appease the abandoned spouses. Remember, for every deed and word man utters, he will give account on the day of Judgment (Matthew 12:36, Romans 2:6). The Lord will never leave us or forsake us, but clearly, man can abandon God with dire consequences (Hebrews 13:5). At the end of a wedding ceremony, the minister proclaims, "What God hath joined together let no man put asunder" (Matthew 19:6). God leaves little room for divorce, and usually, it is sin that destroys a marriage.

More sin in our lives will do us no good. Allowing the ways of the world into a marriage will surely pull on the bonds of a couple's union. The ideal is a happy marriage that lasts a lifetime, which is very rare these days. It does not help for women to go on television and roll their eyes when predicting how long a marriage can last now because of the extended life spans today. Rolling of the eyes or side-eye as it's called today indicates contempt. For God made marriage to last a lifetime of joy and happiness, not for mankind to turn it into a sentence like being in prison.

Philippians 2:14 instructs us to "Do all things without murmurings or disputing's." What excellent marriage counseling that is, if we could only do it. Hebrews 13:5 tells us to be content with such things as we have. God allows us to be content with everything we have and are. It is much easier for Satan to pull us down if we play into his hands by becoming dissatisfied with what God has chosen to provide us with. One good example is the Israelites in the desert complaining about the manna.

We simply cannot change some things in life. Our gender is one of them. Allowing Satan to stir us up as malcontents is not going to benefit anyone except Satan for both sexes have their parts to fulfill in life. Neither sex has it any easier than the other. Both must strive to coexist. In order to do so, anything that pits them against each other must be avoided like the plague. Everything written here in this material can be applied to both sexes, save that the man is the head of the woman. Nothing here is biased or based on gender; instead, it is founded on the Word of God.

In Genesis 2:18 God says, "It is not good that the man should be alone." It is also not good for the women. Studies dating back to the ancient Greeks have proven this.[12] Single men do not live as long as their married counterparts. "But married men are more willing to die."[13]

Studies have proven that hermits live even shorter lives than single men. Single men fail at business enterprises far more often than married men do. It is true that behind every great man there is a woman.

Proverbs 18:22 says, "Whoso findeth a wife findeth a good thing, and obtaineth favor of the Lord." I have never been very good at reading God's mind, but this seems to say He made good women to be blessings to men. James 1:17 tells us all good things come from God. Keeping sin from our lives will fulfill God's plans for us and keep His blessings in our lives. This scripture begs the question: "Is a woman who serves Satan, a good thing?" A good wife will contribute to her husband's journey towards heaven. This supports and defines why God commands not to be married to a non-believer. She will turn her husband away from God and will bring death and destruction as happened to the Israelites. She is not a good wife and does not deserve to be compared to one. The same applies to a Christian woman who is only concerned about her own interests as the worldly feminists teach.

Recent studies have determined that marriage will not make you happy; happiness has to come from within.[14] People are no more satisfied after marriage than they were prior to marriage. Looking for someone else to make you happy will only put a strain on your marriage. The people who were satisfied with their lives before they said, "I do" were more likely to remain married longer. All too often that desire to make the honeymoon happiness last forever leads to divorce. I wish it were possible, but it is just an unrealistic expectation.

Money and sex are two major hurdles to a successful marriage as is communication and maturity. Money is a source of trouble because there is never enough of it. The more you make, the more you spend. To have a happy marriage, learn to communicate with your spouse. It may not last if you do not. Ephesians 4:26 "Be ye angry, and sin not: let not the sun go down upon your wrath." Work out your grievances/differences and do not let things build within you. Learn how to take and give constructive criticism and treat your partner with respect. Respect in marriage is a big word. As I said earlier, if a person does not respect you, he or she is likely to cheat on you.

Those who know how to argue without hurting one another and how to resolve their disagreements are almost guaranteed long and happy marriages according to researchers from Fuller Theological Seminary in Pasadena, Calif., reports Health Day News. In contrast, the No. 1 sign that couples are headed for divorce – even before they walk down the aisle – is that they make negative comments about the relationship or each other.

One secret weapon for a happy, successful marriage is to develop empathy with/for your spouse. This is the ability to sense intellectually and emotionally the emotions, feelings, and reactions that another person is experiencing and to communicate that understanding to the person effectively.

DIVORCE

The National Institutes of Health has determined that almost half of all U.S. marriages end in divorce. Divorce causes more than just bitterness and broken hearts. The trauma can leave long-lasting effects on mental and physical health that remarriage might not repair. according to research. "People who lose a marriage take such damage to their health," said Linda Waite, a sociologist at the University of Chicago in Illinois.

Waite and co-author Mary Elizabeth Hughes, of Johns Hopkins Bloomberg School of Public Health, found that divorced or widowed people have 20 percent more chronic health conditions such as heart disease, diabetes or cancer than married people. Their article, published in the Journal of Health and Social Behavior, examined the marital history and health indicators for 8,652 middle-aged people in research funded by the National Institute on Aging. The authors found differences between the overall health of those who remain married and those who divorce.

"Losing a marriage or becoming widowed or divorced is extremely stressful," Waite said. It's usually financially ruinous for all involved. It's socially extremely difficult. What's interesting is if people have remarried, we still see, in their health, the scars or marks – the damage that was done by this event.

People who have divorced "have more chronic conditions, more mobility limitations, rate their health as poorer than people like them in age, race, gender, education who've been married once and are still married," Waite said. Previous research has suggested that marriage has protective health benefits by providing financial, social, and emotional stability. Married women have more financial security, which means better access to health care and reduced stress, Waite said. "Married men have better health habits," she said in comparison to single males. "They lead a cleaner, healthier life, and spend less time in bars and eat better. Women tend to manage men's interactions with the medical system. Spouses check up on each other's needs."

Those who did not remarry after a divorce or a spouse's death showed deficits in mental and physical health. Waite called this the "double whammy" because they don't get the protective effects of marriage and have gone through a "damaging, health-destroying experience." They had worse health indicators than people who never married; therefore, "didn't get the goods and didn't get the bad," Waite said.

Both genders suffer irreversible, detrimental effects on their health after a divorce or death of a spouse, according to the findings. People who remarried had better health than those who did not. "If you loved and lost, did you find love again?" Waite said. "The people who did are doing better." But this group overall showed health deficits compared to those who remained married.

Mark Hayward, director of the Population Research Center and a professor of sociology Fellow at the University of Texas at Austin, said spouses check up on each other's needs. They remind each other of when to go see a doctor, a dentist or when to get a medical issue checked out. "You're making decisions together about your lifestyle and investing in the future together," said Hayward, who was not involved in the latest research. He found that divorce has a lasting impact on cardiovascular diseases, even after remarriage. His 2006 study, funded by the National Institute on Aging, found that divorced middle-aged women were 60 percent more likely to have cardiovascular disease than middle-aged women who remain married.

"There's no erasure of the effects of divorce," Hayward said. "There is intense stress leading up to the divorce, stresses during divorce proceedings. Think of divorce as one of the most intense stressors. It leads to what we call dysregulation [impairment] in a key cardiovascular process that may be permanently altered. You're not going back to your original set point."

Statistics indicate that the church-going population suffers the same percentage of divorces as the average world population.[15] With the number one cause being adultery. This is very wrong for a group that is supposed to be set aside from the world. We are supposed to be different from the world. As Christians, we are to inherit the kingdom of God. Sadly, even within the church, living for God is sometimes mocked. Something is very wrong with that. If the world mocks you, rejoice because you know you are living right. They even mocked Jesus.

Christians do divorce at the same rate today as the rest of the world but for different causes. Research done by Barna Research Group confirms this and provides other data. The reasons Christians divorce are different from those of the world. The study found that the number one cause in the general population was incompatibility, which Christians rarely use. Christian grounds tend to be adultery, abuse (physical and verbal), and abandonment.[16] The large increase in the divorce rate in recent years came between the years 1960 and 1980.[15] Could the hippies of the sixties' free love have had any responsibility for this? Furstenberg (1994) [17]notes that the United States has one of the highest divorce rates in the world and that this rate has continuously grown over the past 140 years. He suggests that this pattern is connected to the high cultural value that Americans place on independence. He asserts that a culture that values independence encourages people to seek their own personal development, rather than stay committed to family. If you need to be that independent, do not get married in the first place. It just is not fair to your spouse. This is in total contrast to God's doctrine. We do not have to wait until we reach heaven's gates to reap the rewards of our disregard for Him.

Despite what you believe, you are not out of adolescence until age 22 to 24. Do not be in a hurry to get married just because you are legally old enough. The number of divorces today should convince you that marriage is not a walk in the park.

God gives few scriptural reasons for divorce and forbids it for any other cause. I once met a woman who had gotten a divorce because her husband's paycheck was not large enough. I asked her what she had done to encourage or inspire him to better himself. Her answer of nothing came as no surprise to me.

Divorce does not bring financial independence to women. The number one motive women give for filing for welfare is divorce. Divorce is ugly whether it is scriptural or not. I have yet to meet a mother who was happy to raise her children alone. Then why do so many marriages end in divorce? Other than what Charles Stanley (In Touch Ministry) says, "When we get outside the will of God we mess up our lives," I cannot explain why. Perhaps, it is called sin that ruins so many marriages!

I have little doubt that we are in the last times and 2 Timothy 3:2 says in these days men shall be lovers of themselves. We are made in the image of God; therefore, we should have the love for one another as Jesus did when He died for us. The contrast is that Satan only has a love for himself. Marriage is a great chance to love someone else, and selfish love will only ruin your marriage. Being a woman is about what you can do and not what you are due. Do everything for the glory of God, not womankind as the wrong feminists would have you do. I heard a pastor on the radio say, "That submission is simply the way you live your life." Submit to Christ, and He will set you free from Satan's deceit.

A 2011 study by the University of Wisconsin-Madison found that children of divorced parents often fall behind their classmates in math and social skills and are more likely to suffer anxiety, stress, and low self-esteem.

In 1990, Jane Mauldon of the University of California at Berkeley found that children of divorced parents run a 35 percent risk of developing health problems, compared with a 26 percent risk among all children. She thinks their susceptibility to illness is likely due to "very significant stress" as their lives change dramatically.

A 2010 study found that more than 78 percent of children in two-parent households graduated from high school by the age of 20. However, only 60 percent of those who went through a big family change including divorce, death or remarriage graduated in the same amount of time. The younger a child is during the divorce, the more he or she may be affected. The more change children go through, like a divorce followed by a remarriage, the more difficulty they may have finishing school.

In 2009, the law firm Mishcon de Reya polled 2,000 people who had experienced divorce as children in the preceding 20 years. The results did not paint a positive picture of their experiences. The subjects reported witnessing aggression (42 percent), were forced to comfort an upset parent (49 percent) and had to lie for one or the other (24 percent). The outcome was that one in 10 turned to crime and 8 percent considered suicide.

University of Utah researcher Nicholas H. Wolfinger in 2005 released a study showing that children of divorce are more likely to divorce as adults. Despite aspiring to stable relationships, children of divorce are more likely to marry as teens, as well as marry someone who also comes from a divorced family. This suggests that couples in which one spouse has divorced parents may be up to twice as likely to divorce. If both partners experienced divorce as children, they are three times more likely to divorce. Wolfinger said one of the reasons is that children from unstable families are more likely to marry young. (Seeking stability in their lives before finding their own way?)

In the March 2013 edition of *Public Health*, researchers at the University of Toronto found that both sons and daughters of divorced families are significantly more likely to begin smoking than peers whose parents are married.

And rounding out this dreary research is an eight-decade study and book called *The Longevity Project* by Howard Friedman and Leslie Martin. Starting in 1921, researchers tracked some 1,500 boys and girls throughout their lives. More than one-third of the participants experienced either parental divorce or the death of a parent before the age of 21. But it was only the children of divorced families who died on average almost five years earlier than children whose parents did not divorce.

The deaths were from causes both natural and unnatural, but men were more likely to die of accidents or violence. Generally, divorce lowered the standard of living for the children, which made a particular difference in the life longevity of women.

PARENTING

There once was a young lady who had to be dragged to church because she hated it. Of course, when she was old enough she left the church. Then she became entangled in the ways of the world. Just as Proverbs 22:6 says, after a few years, she realized she was not living right and returned to church.

Foolishness is bound in the heart of a child; but the rod of correction shall drive it far from him (Proverbs 22:15).

Researchers at the University of Georgia discovered that girls who attended church services regularly worked more hours during a year of work – eighty more hours for Catholics and almost twice that for Protestants. Can't help but wonder what they would find if they had studied about their ethics regarding sex. Clearly, bringing children to church regularly will have a lifelong influence on them. "Train up a child in the way he should go: and when he is old, he will not depart from it" (Proverbs 22:6).

A study published in the Archives of Pediatrics & Adolescent Medicine stated that only one-third of preteens and young teens were having sex by the two-year mark after having 8 to 12 hours of abstinence training. Comparing this to the 50% who were active after only safe sex instruction, indicates that abstinence training works. And it was not religiously based. Shame on us Christians if we cannot do better.

I know that elsewhere I compared children to Adam and Eve when they were in the garden and still sinless. I maintain that

116

God is not willing that any should perish and did not create anyone destined for hell (II Peter 2:9). The trouble comes with our sin nature that we are all born with or foolishness as the above scripture proclaims. It is your job as a parent to see that this foolishness is driven from your children and that they become the way God desires them to be. You will not achieve this trying to be their best friend. I can still vividly remember the pained expression on my son's face when I had to tell him I was not his best friend; I was his father. After telling him "that was better" his expression picked up. Your friends are not supposed to give you likings.

Withhold not correction from the child: for if thou beatest him with the rod, he shall not die. Thou shalt beat him with the rod, and shalt deliver his soul from hell (Proverbs 23:13-14).

Parents who believe in free will to raise their children are turning from God's instructions and as we see in this scripture will deliver their children to hell. As Christians, we should recognize that every time man has deviated from God's instructions, it has had dire consequences throughout biblical times and our lives.

He that spareth his rod hateth his son: but he that loveth him chasteneth him betimes (Proverbs 13:24).

Sparing the rod spoils the child. When you see a grown man have a temper tantrum just like a six-year-old, you will realize what sparing the rod can do. I know because I asked his mother if she had given him any lickings when he was little. Her answer of "no" came as no surprise to me. Proverbs 18:18 instructs us to "Chasten thy son while there is hope, and let not thy soul spare for his crying." I heard a minister on the radio say if you are spanking them when they are teenagers, it is probably too late.

Freud divided our personalities into three separate structures: the id, the ego, and the super-ego. He considered the id the infant within us that persist throughout life. The id wants to obtain pleasure immediately and avoid pain at all costs. Then again, some adults just get credit cards.

The ego is the rational part that mediates between the id and reality. It anticipates the consequences of particular means of gratification, even delaying gratification. Learning that we can get burned if we play with fire is the ego's responsibility. Problems will persist into adult life if the pains of corporal punishment are removed as mentioned above. Children left to their own devices will run astray every time. Parents who believe in raising children with free will are setting themselves up for failure.

Never forget that we were created in God's image and are capable of the same kind of love just not as much of it. Jesus died for everyone; we certainly cannot love that much. Have God's love towards your children as He has for you in Hebrews 12:6, "For whom the Lord loveth he chasteneth, and scourgeth every son whom he receiveth."

Fathers, provoke not your children to anger, lest they be discouraged (Colossians 3: 21).

Keep your punishment just, and your children will never grow to hate you or be discouraged. Use kindness and gentleness when asserting your authority over them. This will make it easier for them to fulfill God's commandment to honor their parents. Never belittle your children; that is just plain bad parenting. Remember you were young once too. I recently went to a concert where one of the female lead singers was only 15 years old. I can think of many others who have accomplished such things early in their lives. I wish I had the opportunity to ask each of them if their parents ever told them, "You'll never amount to anything. "I sincerely doubt they ever did because when an authority figure says that to a child, it will probably come true.

"The rod and reproof give wisdom: but a child left to himself bringeth his mother to shame" (Proverbs 29:15). Failing to follow God's instructions will be reflected in your children when they become adults. It should come as no surprise if parents are not involved in their children's lives that they will follow the ways of the world in all things, especially sex. "A foolish son is the calamity of his father: and the contentions of a wife are a continual dropping" (Proverbs 19:13). Even on television now, ads prompt parents to be involved in their children's lives because it will help keep them off drugs.

In one commercial, a mother was talking to her child about smoking while he was still in a high chair. It is never too early, just too late to be there for your children. This was never truer than when an eight-year-old girl propositioned me as a grown man to have sex with her.

Even the world has figured out what God says about children left to themselves and implores parents to be involved in their children's lives. Truth is still truth regardless if it comes from a man who figured out God's truths on his own. It should follow that if you need to talk about smoking, drinking, and drugs with your children, it is imperative to discuss sex also. Janet

Rosenbaum, Ph.D., of Johns Hopkins Bloomberg School of Public Health in Baltimore, Maryland, states that "When it comes to advice for the parents of teens, that just about every organization, from Focus on the Family to Planned Parenthood, offers a similar message. "Parents should talk to their kids about their sex. It should not be a single conversation; it should be a continued conversation at the moments that are teachable moments," she says. "Parents tend to hope that schools will take care of it – they can't, obviously."

The number one cause girls gave for having premarital sex was a lack of a good reason not to. They all wonder, "Should I, or shouldn't I?" You had better give them grounds for why they should not. Then you can be proud when you walk your daughter down the aisle and present her to her husband, your new son. She will be a reflection of your parenting, for good or bad. It is up to you.

One more thing about when you walk her down the aisle: before you do, teach her how to manage money. Money will be a big problem in her marriage especially if she has no idea how the bills get paid. Do this, and the chances of her bouncing back into your home will be far less. The boy's also need this instruction.

Today, we have the term rebound babies, boomerang kids, the Peter Pan Generation – but regardless of what they're called, adult children are moving back home in droves. There are many reasons for it, but it seems they won't leave either. Have a daughter? If she returns because of divorce, don't be surprised if she has a few kids in tow. If that happens to you, ask yourself if you taught her how to stand on her own two feet. Was it also from habitually making poor dating choices? From my personal observation, the females are more likely to become like the males than the other way around. So, you want to be influential in your daughter's dating choices as well as your son's! With divorce rates above 50%, many newly-separated spouses have nowhere else to go but home to Mom and Dad.

"Fathers provoke not your children to anger lest they become discouraged" (Colossians 4:21). This scripture begs the question: "How do you provoke your children to anger?"

- You constantly belittle and ridicule them.
- You do not include them in things because you simply do not want to deal with them.
- You expect too much from them and let them know how much they failed you.

That will do it. Your children will seek out a spouse like that because we all tend to gravitate towards what is normal whether it is good for us or not. We are not capable of making our own decisions until we are 18, so a child's choices are not likely to be good ones. The older your children are, walking them through the decision process rather than just making it for them is a good idea.

More than ever, today, our children are bombarded with information that is not all good. The problem is that during adolescence, they are limited in their abilities to make decisions on their own. Some researchers define late adolescence as nineteen through twenty-one. Yes, I remember saying that we are not out of adolescence until age 24, and I stand by it. The feminists also erroneously equate a teen to being a young woman. What teenager would not eat that up? All too often, they mistakenly think they are adults if they can do some adult things. Like, have sex. Recently, I read somewhere in the media where an eight-year-old was called a young woman. How mistaken is that?

My reasoning for including this is because the feminists are not only invading college campuses but are organizing high school students as well as churches. Let this serve as a warning to you as parents that you must be vigilant in being involved in your children's lives.

The ungodly feminists and their lesbian agenda are preying upon our children, and I correctly fear they are being brainwashed. Make no mistake about it; these sexual deviates are at work on both you and your children through these feminists.

As a parent, you need to know that the feminists fight for over the counter contraceptives that your children can buy without your knowledge. They also vindictively fight the "Child Custody Protection Act" passed by Congress that forbids a teen from getting an abortion in another state without her parent's knowledge. Of course, that is why they want to go to another state so their parents may never find out.

In short, they encourage your teenage daughters to be sexually active under your roof and believe that you have no say in the matter. I have yet to see where they discuss S.T.D's or tell them that the only foolproof way to avoid pregnancy is abstinence.

One very good and effective method of raising gentlemen and ladies is to call your children just that. It gives them a path they will want to follow. It definitely will provide them with a higher regard for self. I once met someone who introduced his two daughters to me as his "monsters." He was right too. I suggested he call them ladies for a while and watch the changes it would make in them. About two months later, he sent me a message that they had improved a lot. He said they did not think he cared, so they did not bother behaving. Not only did this show them he cared but it gave them a path to follow as they grew. I distinctly remember being in a store one day when a woman with two daughters referred to them as ladies when it was time to go. It is time for more mothers to do the same.

I know from experience that you can inspire four-year-olds to desire to become ladies. Just explain that not every girl grows up to be a lady, and those who do are valued above the rest – just like rubies. Your daughters must act like little ladies first and not worry about the grown-up rules. Simply be little girls and have all the fun they can. Tell them they can't just say, "I am a lady."

Naturally, most parents want their daughters to get the best husbands they can find. As parents, you need to work at making your daughter the best she can be. To catch the best husband, you will need to have some really good bait. Also, do not forget to work on making your sons into the best husbands they can be.

Current research shows that girls as young as 11 are having issues with their bodies. Many young girls suffer from the Princess Syndrome (PS) daily. A girl who suffers from PS lives life as a fairy-tale: focusing only on the pretty things, putting herself at the center of the universe, and obsessing about her looks. While this can be fun and whimsical when a girl is a toddler, it can also set the tone for how she develops into a young woman, influencing her self-esteem, her dependence on others, and how she takes care of herself. Expecting your daughter, at age 3, 4, or 5 to understand that life is better if you have solid values, good friends, and a healthy lifestyle, in comparison to the princess lifestyle, is unrealistic. It is up to you, as a parent, to combat the pressures coming from the outside.

She will likely learn that she cannot be self-sufficient and that she has to rely on a savior to make it all better. This can include friendships that are uninspiring and superficial and a lack of internal drive because she "expects" it all to come to her. Where do you start? Your first instinct may be to try to shield your daughter. Unfortunately, this is virtually impossible. Instead, teach her how to deal with any pressure and help her develop her own self-image that builds a healthy self-esteem. Starting young, as I've said, can set the stage for your daughter as she grows up. Definitely, teach her about dressing properly and make her aware of advertising messages. Teach your daughter to be an educated consumer.

In Chapter 2 of I Samuel, we see that the priest Eli's sons caused the women of Israel to sin by having sex with them. Even though Eli entreats them, he never stops them. In verse 27, a man of God came to Eli and proclaimed God's anger and punishment to both Eli and his sons. In verse 34, Eli is told that both his sons shall die in one day. Earlier in verses 30 & 31, God tells Eli what shall happen to him for despising God by not restraining his sons. God says in verses 31 & 32: "There shall not be an old man in thine house forever." All Eli's descendants are going to die at a young age because Eli has not performed as a parent to keep his sons in the ways of the Lord.

In Chapter 3 of 1 Samuel, God calls to Samuel three times and each time; he runs to Eli thinking it is he who has called him. Realizing it is the Lord calling, Eli instructs Samuel to say, "Speak Lord for thy servant heareth." In verse 13, God proclaims to Samuel that He will judge Eli's house forever because his sons made themselves vile and he restrained them not. The importance here is Eli's punishment for not stopping his sons from sinning with the women who gathered at the temple door. Verse 14 of the said chapter shows that this curse shall not be removed with any amount of sacrifice or offering.

It cannot be said too many times that sex is a really big thing to God. It certainly is a big device of Satan's. Even though Eli did not commit the sin of fornication, as a parent, he was held responsible for his sons' actions because he turned a blind eye to their sins. Simply chastising them as in verses 23 & 24 of Chapter 2 was not sufficient to prevent God's punishment. Just because they were his children was not enough, and clearly, his example did not restrain them. He failed to take the time to be in their lives and take action.

This undoubtedly makes for a profound impact on the parents of today. Can we weasel out of this if we can say we are not men of God? We may not reap the same punishment as Eli did on his descendants but this speaks clearly that as parents, we can still pay for our children's sins if we are not actively molding them with God's laws.

Naturally, the question comes to mind as to exactly when to tell a young lady about the birds and the bees. I personally believe not before the age of 10 and not after 12. All children not being equal, there is not likely a definite number to throw out. However, on this subject, I would like to share a couple of personal incidents and let you, the parent, decide. As we all know, children learn a lot of things outside the home. When one mother went to talk with her twelve-year-old, the child asked the mother what she wanted to know. She had already learned about sex from her friends.

When I was a senior in high school, during gym, the 7th and 8th graders were also there with us. Somehow, one of the twelve-year-old girls started a conversation with me that eventually revealed how two of her male classmates had conducted a little experiment with her in the bathroom. She did not even realize that they had had sex with her. If you do not want your twelve-year-olds to know about sex, find some way of making sure they do not participate in any experiments that could not be done in public.

I cannot overemphasize the importance of providing reasons to abstain from premarital sex when talking to your children. A woman brought her thirteen-year-old daughter to work quite frequently, and it became apparent to me that she needed to speak to her about sex. Her mother asked me why, and I told her "Boys" then I told her about the above-mentioned twelve-year-old. Apparently, she also told her daughter that story because when the truth finally came out, this thirteen-year-old took two of her male classmates into the bathroom. When you do talk to them, this is an excellent example of why you need to have reasons for them not to.

It is your decision when to tell your children about sex. These are some of my experiences, and I hope they will help you make your decision. I believe that in order to be involved in your children's choices about sex, you must be able to talk to them about it openly and comfortably. What child fully comprehends sex? A lot of adults do not either. If you let your kids play with fire, you are a terrible parent. Do everything you can to keep your kids from playing with sex. This book is truly meant to liberate our young from Satan's device called sex. If you, as a parent, can figure out how to get children grow up right without telling them what to do and not do, please let me know.

You should tell them that the best time for them to have sex is on their wedding night and every time they have sex before marriage is just another flaw within them. Make it very clear that once they start, they will find it difficult if not impossible to ever stop. Also, tell them it will not make an adult out of them. This applies to both sexes, so talk to your sons and your daughters. The thing that will have the single most crucial influence on this matter is to teach your sons to value a woman's virtue.

Surely, too many young ladies mistakenly believe it is them, not sex that young men are after. I remember one seventeen-year-old female who had sex because a classmate claimed that if they did, he would marry her. Needless to say, no male in high school was interested in marriage, but she believed him anyway. I can still vividly picture her crying when she found out she had been fooled. No, this is not a confession; it was not me.

As James 1:8 says, "A double minded man is unstable in all his ways." When talking to your children about sex do not waver. Tell him or her there is no temptation that they cannot overcome to abstain from premarital sex (1 Corinthians 10:13). They look to you as their example. You will not succeed if you appear doubtful that they can overcome. Tell them there is no reason they cannot resist temptation firmly and always. Show them Philippians 4:13: "I can do all things through Christ which strengtheneth me," and they will gain confidence. Be firm, as you must be to lead your children down the path of righteousness.

Point out that there is no cause for them to have premarital sex and temptation is not justification. I was discussing a 12-year-old with her mother one day when the mother asked me if I thought her daughter could save herself until her marriage. Not knowing that the daughter was listening, I said: "In this world today, it is inevitable that she will fail." Having overheard this, it turned out I was right. Leave no room for doubt, and you will be well equipped to succeed.

It is my hope that the material in this book will help your daughters and sons understand the value of girls being true ladies. If we do not show them we care, it is unlikely that our young women will care either. Likely if parents do not care enough to discuss this, how can their children be expected to care? This applies to other aspects of children's lives, such as schoolwork. Surveys show that a girl is less likely to have premarital sex (or more likely to start later) if her mother is more involved in her life.

It is demonstrated in Deuteronomy Chapter 22 that sex before marriage just one time makes a girl a whore. Then there seems to be what the world classifies as a whore. Which is more important to you: God's definition of a whore or the world's? What does the way you dress say about you? It is my observation and opinion that a girl who starts having sex at a young age is more/most likely to become a whore by the world's standards. Not to be a bore by repeating myself but as Christians, we are to march to the beat of a different drummer and not conform to the world's standards. Nevertheless, no matter which drummer you march to, being involved in your daughter's life will have a life-long impact on her. If you don't play a major role in your children's lives, the world will step in and take your place. Being their source of information about sex will give you the ability to influence them to make godly decisions.

It is more important to guide and lead children than to try to force or control them. Children become more independent as they get older and want to make decisions on their own. Trying to make decisions for them without reasoning will lead to rebellion. Guiding them through the decision process will prove far more effective. One thing this book is designed to do is to make them want to be victorious over the world by not just focusing on the consequences of falling. Herein is the basis, which God has for you to inspire and lead your children. If you cannot use the guidelines in this book to successfully guide your daughters, then you never will and had better break out those proverbial boards of cedar.

Once, at a church gathering, a little girl sat beside me, but her parents wanted her to sit with them. She refused. I told her about Ephesians 1:4 where God knew her before He made the world. Then I told her he had picked her parents for her since He knew them as well and wondered if she thought He had made a bad choice. She got mad at me. Then I asked her why she talked to them and disobeyed them the way she did if she thought God made a good choice in making them her parents. I told her to honor her parents by the way she talked to them and to do what they said. Use this example to teach children why God commands them to honor their parents.

In the seventeenth century, a chastity belt was used to keep foolish maidens from giving away their virtue. Some parents today will go so far as to inform their daughters that if they flaw themselves and lose their virtue, their father may not walk them down the aisle at their wedding. This may seem cruel, but if you wish to instill the values of decency in your children, you need to let them know how much you value it yourself.

Some parents falsely believe that their children will turn out all right simply because they are their children and they, as parents, are setting a good example. Unfortunately, "Every way of a man is right in his own eyes" (Proverbs 21:2a). I cannot overemphasize the importance and need for parents to spend the time necessary to instruct their children. Helping a child reach his or her full potential requires effort on the part of the parents. Setting goals and making plans to achieve them by utilizing all methods available are better than leaving it up to the children to figure out on their own. We know that they will run astray on their own every time. We must give our children the full armor of God and an overwhelming desire to stand firm. (See Appendix C for a description of God's Armor.)

Our children are reflections of ourselves as I've stated elsewhere. That's why some parents always want the smartest kid, a beauty queen or a winning athlete. Wanting to live life vicariously through them is not suitable for the children. They need and want unconditional love, which will make for happy and well-adjusted adults. Let us remember that we were created in God's image and that His love is boundless, as should ours for our children be also. It is time for adults to consider their children's morals as reflections of themselves.

Never underestimate the importance of telling your children that you love them. Even God told His Son that He was beloved by Him in Luke 9:35: "And there came a voice out of the cloud, saying, "This is my beloved Son: hear him." We don't always figure things out on our own and sometimes, need to be told. Deeds alone may not be enough for children to understand that they are, indeed, loved.

Many young girls will use sex to feel special to a male figure especially if they lack a father's love in their lives. This lack of love can happen even if her father is present in her life. Also referred to as present but absent. Then some guys will compliment a girl when she is very young to get her to have sex with them. If this succeeds, you are easy no matter what your age.

For about a year, my former wife and I took care of a ten-year-old girl and her younger brother. Years later, as an adult, she once asked me, "How did you get me to love you?" I replied that just like God, I had loved her first. "We love him because he first loved us" (I John 4:19). Love your children, and they will want your presence over any gift you could ever give them. Some psychologists believe that how adults develop love relationships is directly linked to how their parents related to them in early childhood. People with a secure handle of love described their parents as warm and supportive; those with anxious and avoidant styles described their parents as demanding, critical, and uncaring. Love is indeed taught.

A holy man's children are blessed when his righteousness has influenced their lives (Proverbs 20:7). Children's children are the crown of old men (Proverbs 17:6). It is an honor to you when your grandchildren are influenced by the godly influence you had on their parents. That does not mean you are done because you are still a strong influence in your grandchildren's lives. I still remember many, if not all, of the lessons my grandfather taught me when I was young.

Children are your legacy to the world. Do you want to leave behind young men and women who are ladies and gentlemen for God? Psalms 127:3 pronounces children as a heritage from the Lord. "Be not deceived; God is not mocked: for whatsoever a man soweth, that shall he also reap" (Galatians 6:7). I have met several older people who lamented how their children did not visit them enough. Each one that I have asked how much they were involved in their children's lives could not tell me "a lot." Parents who often argue have weaker relationships with their children (Amato & Sobolewski, 2001).

Children whose parents often argue score worse on measures of academic achievement, behavior problems, psychological well-being, and adult relationship quality; they are also more likely to form families early and outside of marriage (Amato PR, Sobolewski JM)

It is also a great help if our young men are taught to desire, value, and seek out virtuous women. We must teach our sons to avoid women of low reputation, and teach our daughters not to ridicule or mock a young man who does value virtue in women. After all, who likes to be embarrassed? Reject a man, and it is all over. Men would rather be alone than ridiculed, humiliated, and rejected. Little wonder those feminists teach their followers how to get rid of a man and make sure he never comes back. They desire to turn them into men haters as well as men chasers. Is this the height of what it means to be a woman?

Make sure you are in your children's lives. Young girls who lack a father figure in their lives will seek that out in their adulthood by using sex. Boys will act out even though they know they will get into trouble just for a male presence in their lives. One child of an unwed mother threw a rock at my car just to get a male presence in his life no matter what. I pray every night before I go to bed, but one night I got down on my knees next to my bed and prayed. I have not done that since I was a kid. What brought me to that position? Two little girls. I was grocery shopping, and there was a woman with her two girls in the shopping cart. I ran into them in two aisles, and each time the little girls kept calling me poppy. "Hello, poppy," they said pleadingly. It was apparent to me that they must not have a father in their lives. That made me sad, especially that they would reach out to a total stranger for a substitute. Ask yourself if this is what you want for your daughters?

I helped one 10-year-old girl with her homework once. She broke down and cried when I asked her why she said her father did not help her with her homework. Even if you are not an absentee father, you can still be missing in action when it comes to your daughter.

I once attended a church where the pastor had three daughters. I still remember him stating from the pulpit, "God help you if you have girls." I think this problem is termed "Boy Crazy." This term means she is crazy about boys in general. For many young girls, this is just a normal and harmless phase, which parents must deal with. Others must face the more destructive behaviors associated with being boy crazy, such as lying, sneaking out to meet boys and the consequences of sexual activity at a young age. Children are great imitators of their parents so if you are a single mother, practice what you expect from your daughter. If your daughter is focusing on one particular boy that is not being boy crazy, but she still needs your guidance on what is proper and acceptable behavior. Apply the material in this book.

Fill her time with constructive and meaningful activities. Find her a hobby if she does not already have one and help her to become involved in activities at school, church or the community. By focusing her mind on other interests, she has less time for obsessing over boys. Spend time with your daughter by doing activities and going places, she likes. Often, girls become boy crazy because they lack attention at home and the attention they receive from boys helps to fill this need. Don't underestimate the importance of this either. A young boy who is actively being pursued by a crazy girl is a recipe for disaster.

Parents need to handle situations like these because a girl without limitations will lead to certain disaster if they don't. Do not leave children to their own devices. Set curfews and enforce them. Also, limit her use of phones, social media and other means of association with boys on a regular basis. When it comes time to let her date, prevent her from serial dating and boys you feel are not good for her. Ensure that her friends are not also boy crazy.

Want well-behaved children? Concentrate on what they watch on television. Researchers report in the journal *Pediatrics* on their success in helping parents to increase the time kids spent watching educational programming. The result? Better- behaved children. They also suggest you watch these programs with them. In doing so, you will be able to interpret anything they don't understand. Children are sponges that absorb their surroundings and imitate their parents.

In 2007, the American Psychological Association's Task Force on the Sexualization of Girls issued a report linking early sexualization with three of the most common mental-health problems of girls and women: eating disorders, low self-esteem, and depression. There's nothing inherently wrong with parents wanting to appease their daughters by buying them the latest fashions. But is getting cool points today worth the harm dressing little girls like prostitutes could cause tomorrow?

WHAT YOUR MOTHER DID NOT TELL YOU ABOUT SEX

Sex outside of marriage before or after can destroy a marriage. Even so-called open marriages do not work. Premarital sex will taint both partners and weaken the marital bonds. I hope this statement stirs up some kind of reaction within you. Let me enlighten you as to why premarital sex will undermine any marriage. First Corinthians 6:16 and Genesis 2:24 state that two shall be one flesh, referring to sex as a union of two souls in these scriptures.

In biblical times, marriages consisted of a one-year engagement, then a gathering, ending in the bride and groom going into their marriage tent to consummate their marriage. The marriage ceremony we have today did not originate with Adam and Eve. It was the Romans who first turned it into a ritual. Every time you have sex before your marriage you are joining your body and soul to a person other than your spouse just like in the ancient marriage ceremony. In short, you are giving him or her part of your soul. "What? Know ye not that he, which is joined to an harlot, is one body? for two, saith he, shall be one flesh" (1 Corinthians 6:16). This Scripture is not referring to the physical aspect of sex but to the spiritual joining of souls. Consequently, when you give yourself to someone in premarital sex, you will have less of your soul to give to your future husband. This applies to men as well. A man will have less to give to his wife as well.

I like to compare this to the chemical bonding of atoms to create a compound. The man and the woman in this analogy would represent two atoms. If they are joined in a strong (pure) bond, they will become difficult, if not impossible, to separate. However, if it is a weak bond, then separation is likely. So, it is with marriage today.

Premarital sex will weaken the union of two souls and make it increasingly difficult for their bond (marriage) to survive the troubles of today's world. It is not just sex after all. On a couple's wedding night, every person they have both slept with will be there with them also. It is far better to keep guilt out of your marriage; for guilt will interfere with a married couple's sex life.

Sex before marriage can also confuse you as to whether what you feel about this person is real love or just lust. I have witnessed couples whose relationship is based on lust, and after the physical attraction wears off, they realize too late that they no longer truly love each other. If some men do fall in love over sex, after the excitement wears off, they will get bored with you and go looking for another conquest, even if you did get married. That is lust, not real lasting love.

If a guy tells you that you have something special, ask to see the ring. Because having sex is nothing special; any female can do that. Marriage is something special because it says to the world we have reserved ourselves for each other. If a man really loves you, he will wait for you until your wedding night.

I worked with a woman whose boyfriend had told her he would not see her anymore unless they had sex. I told her that if he really loved her, he would not say that. Later, she angrily informed me that if she had waited another week, she would have lost him.

Years later, I met her again, and she introduced me to her husband. I asked if he was the boyfriend she had when I saw her last. He was not, and she was so embarrassed I knew she had sex with another man that she immediately had to leave. Do not embarrass yourself like this when you stand before God's throne or your husband on your wedding night.

Who can find a virtuous woman? for her price is far above rubies. The heart of her husband doth safely trust in her, so that he shall have no need of spoil (Proverbs 31:10-11).

When her husband is away, his heart will trust in her because she will tend to his business as he would. A virtuous woman will not spoil anything of her husband's including herself. It would be ludicrous to think that adultery and premarital sex will not spoil their marriage. A smart man married to a virtuous woman will value his wife above rubies. A wise husband will know this and value his wife above money, and it will make him more content than having any amount of money ever could.

A woman who comes to her husband pure on their wedding night is far more trustworthy than one who has been spoiled by premarital sex. She will be far more valuable too; men do not seek out prostitutes to marry. "no need of spoil" refers to her behavior before marriage as well as after. As the late Rex Humbard once said on his television ministry, "If you can't trust them before marriage, you will not be able to trust them after."

Do not use sex to get a man or to keep him. If sex is all you have that will keep a man, then that is all you are and will ever be to him, just a sex object. In the long run, you will end up alone. In the words of the late Ann Landers, "The sample was ample."

It's like in the department stores when they give away a small free sample. More often than not the recipient does not buy the goods. I am sure some of the women reading this are saying that men will not come around if you are not willing to have sex. If a man says he won't date you or fall in love with you without sex, don't be surprised if all he wants is sex. If you give in to this, don't be surprised if he leaves when it gets old to him, or you stop. This would explain why so many guys will disappear when you become pregnant also. Let no one call me sexist. Would you rather be alone and pregnant or just be alone? If you're expecting a baby, you will need to find someone who is willing to accept your tainted love and a child. The reality is that not many young men want an instant family.

Only 8% of married American women are virgins on their wedding night.[1] Sadly, it is only 8% but they saved themselves, and so can other women. There is no justifiable reason you cannot, too. No gentleman would require sex to stay with you before you are married. Never fear the loss of such a man because he will have his own interests in mind over any consideration for you. Appendix A is a comparison of the results of what has happened to two sisters where one did, and the other did not have premarital sex.

There are many myths in regards to sex, some of which I hope to clear up. The Creator, not Satan, gave sex to us. Satan uses it to destroy us. Using sex as a tool and/or a weapon is another way to reduce yourself to a sex object to a man. In plain English, you are making a prostitute of yourself, even to your husband. Searching the Internet, I found a site that proclaims prostitutes commit suicide 45 times more often than the average population. Sex clearly did not do much for them. What makes you think it will work miracles for you if you exploit it or use it in or outside of marriage? Anyway, different from God's designs will bring you down.

Sex is cheapened when it is sold. This does not only refer to when a woman sells her body but also to when she exploits her sex appeal. This can include anything from the way a woman dresses to how she conducts herself to achieve her desires. Pornography is another way a woman exploits her sexuality. "As a jewel of gold in a swine's snout, so is a fair woman, which is without discretion" (Proverbs 11:22). That is indeed a terrible waste.

Hebrews 13:4 says that in marriage, the bed is "undefiled." That means sex with your spouse is sinless, and anything goes, as long as your spouse is consenting. Sex becomes dirty when it is outside of marriage (pre-marital or adulterous) also when you listen to those who believe it is just sex. Sex is a big thing to God. 1 Corinthians 10:8 proves this; it tells of the twenty-three thousand who fell for fornicating.

The marriage bed becomes defiled if one or both partners commit ADULTERY. Pre-marital sex also defiles a marriage. The importance of keeping your marriage bed undefiled both before and during the marriage cannot be overemphasized for both genders. Several books have been written about regaining the lost intimacy of premarital sex in a marriage. It is better never to need those books. I came across this statement while on the internet. "You can never erase or replace the memories from another lover."

Nevertheless to avoid fornication, let every man have his own wife, and let every woman have her own husband. Let the husband render unto the wife due benevolence: and likewise also the wife unto the husband. The wife hath not power of her own body, but the husband: and

likewise also the husband hath not power of his own body, but the wife. Defraud ye not one the other, except it be with consent for a time, that ye may give yourselves to fasting and prayer; and come together again, that Satan tempt you not for your incontinency (1 Corinthians 7: 2-5).

Once again, the equality of a man and his wife is apparent. For both man and woman are to render their bodies to their spouses. To refuse is to allow the tempter to work on your spouse's soul as well as your own and you become Satan's servant. James 1:13 tells us that God does not tempt man; He may test us, as with Job, but He cannot tempt us. But every man is tempted, when he is drawn away of his own lust, and enticed (vs. 14).

When lust conceives, it results in sin (vs. 15). Satan is the father of sin. Never withhold sex from your spouse to get what you want because you are a catcher of souls for Satan when you do.

By putting a price on sex, you have prostituted yourself out to your husband. "Let not sin therefore reign in your mortal body, that ye should obey it in the lusts thereof" (Romans 6:12). By denying your spouse sex, you are allowing Satan to tempt your spouse; you have become his instrument of destruction. Do you expect to escape? I think not. You are to run interference just like a football player for your spouse against the Devil's attacks on him or her. 1 Corinthians 7 applies to both genders. Anything such as feminism that teaches its followers otherwise is clearly the work of Satan. Make no mistake about it.

A married woman who says, "It's my body" is not following God's doctrine. In the same thought, do not equate consensual sex with your husband to rape. Think long and hard about the motives of the feminists who would propagate this folly.

There are only two motives a guy has to ask a female out on a date. Either he just wants sex or is interested in a relationship. Can you say, "I do not do sex before marriage?" Here is a hint: if a man says he just wants one date, it is a good indication that all he wants is sex. Realize that no normal man is going to marry a woman he absolutely does not want to have sex with. Wanting to does not equal trying to. Do not treat a man like he has tried to when he has not. The secular feminists teach this as one more way to alienate you from men with plans to turn you toward your own gender.

Consequently, you are going to have to give men the benefit of the doubt until you feel they have done something inappropriate. A kiss is not inappropriate. However, never participate in other activities that will lead to temptation. When I was a kid every house had one of those two-person swings out on the front yard. That was where the courting went on. It is a natural, God-given response for men and women to desire the opposite sex. In 1 Corinthians 7, some versions refer to this desire as our "natural affection one for another." That means men for women and women for men. Be nice about it; be very nice about it but make it clear that you do not take part in premarital sex. If he comes back, you will know he is not just interested in you for sex.

When you date a man, refrain from telling him you will never have sex with him. Instead, tell him you do not do sex before marriage. Trust me as a man; I know he will take it personally. In other words, do not shoot yourself in the foot and chase a fellow away. I remember watching a young girl saying on TV: "You've got to be nice about it." The 8% of women who remained virgins until they married could not have overdone it. They could not have mocked a man who was willing to wait for them either. No man is going to stick around for a foolish woman who will mock him. Who likes to be embarrassed? For an example of how this can change your chances of marriage see, Appendix A. A man is also not likely to marry a woman who annoys (nags) him before they are married either.

I was talking to one of the pastors at church when a young woman walked up and told the pastor there was someone who wanted to have sex with her. I said there were two things wrong with that and one was that no normal man would marry any woman with whom he did not want to have sex. The pastor agreed with me, and she asked what the other thing was. I replied that wanting to does not equal trying to and that if she acted like every man who wanted to, actually did try to, she would never get to rule number one.

Understand that the first thing a married woman is apt to do when she is mad at her husband is to withhold sex. Some even commit adultery as a means of getting even for the way she perceives she is mistreated by her husband. Women do these things to bruise men's egos by rejection. This does not mean you should have sex before marriage, but hopefully, you now realize that acting as if a man made a pass at you if he has not is a sure sign to him of your rejection. Sorry, but only losers like to be rejected.

Do not fall for the fallacy of equivocation that the secular feminists teach where you think and act like every man wants your body just because if you offered yourself to him, he would accept. The first thing that is wrong with that idea is no woman or man can appeal to every one of the opposite sex. So, there will be some men who would never think of you in that way.

The second and most dangerous aspect of this thinking is that you will eventually run around afraid that every man wants your body. I hope I do not have to tell you what this sounds like, right? So, do not act as if every man has made a pass at you. It is also very sad when all you have that a man would want you for is sex. Or, at least, that is all you think you have that would make him interested in you. Needless to say, this will turn away a lot of men from you and only reinforce the hate relationship between man and woman that is propagated by those feminists. Lastly, if a guy is not interested in you, it does not make him gay. Not every man is ruled by his hormones, and it does matter how you conduct yourself; just look at the number of divorces.

I know a true story of a young man who was willing to travel 6 hours for a woman who had made it very clear that she did not have sex before marriage. Unfortunately, she laughed at him. He asked her why she was saving herself if she mocked a man who desired that quality in her, she could not give him any rationalization. The next time he saw her, he found out that she had given up on saving herself. When she asked him if he was still interested, he said "no." He did not need to travel 6 hours for soiled goods. It is imperative that parents give their daughters valid justification for abstaining, not merely tell them to. I have seen several instances similar to this one. The number one excuse given by girls for not abstaining was the lack of a reason to. I cannot say this enough.

This young woman, without an ulterior motive, obviously could not see a reason to abstain any longer. Plainly, in this case, the adage, "If it's not broke, don't fix it" held too true. This entire book was written to provide parents grounds to give a girl that will help her see why she should abstain and want to do so. The first step is getting her to desire purity.

Then give her rules to follow that will help her to abstain but remember that rules without understanding will lead to failure. Show her I Samuel 15:23: "For rebellion is as the sin of witchcraft, and stubbornness is as iniquity and idolatry." Rebellion against God's design for us will only lead to our downfall.

I also know of a woman who turned down a date with a man because she thought he just wanted her for sex. She ended up with another man. After a while, he told her he had only wanted her for sex and then left her. After this, she went back to the first man, but he was no longer interested in her. He was too insulted and hurt by her. If all he had wanted was sex, this would not have mattered to him.

Romans 1:26 and 27 confirm I Corinthians 7 in that it is perfectly natural for a man to love a woman and for a woman to love a man. Remember this the next time a woman prances around on stage and tells the audience, "It's not natural for a man to love a woman." Romans 1:26 states how even the women changed their natural use. What is their natural use? It can only be the women for the men. Verse 27 further supports the man's natural attraction for a woman when it states the man left the natural use of the woman. Anyone who tells you that this natural attraction of the man to the woman is wrong is turning one of God's truths into a lie. Anyone who believes him or her has been fooled. Ask yourself what motive anyone would have to turn this truth into a lie. Hell is full of fools. Liberate yourselves from the lies of fools and follow God's natural order for man and woman. Furthermore, it is no one else's business what you and your husband do with each other.

Learn to recognize a nice man from all the rest. Men can be divided into two groups: selfless and selfish. Selfish men can be divided again into two categories:

1. Those who will put you down to get what they want.

These are men who will make you feel inferior, so you will do what they really want you to do for them. This is supposed to make you think you will get your dignity back from them. All this will prove is that you are seeking male approval. I am reminded of the word "subservient." Do not fall for this; a smart woman values sex more highly. Never let others control how you feel about yourself. Stand up for yourself because if you stand for nothing, you will fall for anything.

2. The "Mister Slicks" (also known as players).

They will puff themselves up so you will want to be associated with them by giving them sex, which will only make you subservient to them. They may do this by exalting themselves or by putting other men down so you will submit to their manliness. Do not be fooled, especially if the other guy is smaller than the bully. If you get involved with them, all you will have is a selfish man. Nice men will not put you or anyone else down. So, if you find one, let him know you appreciate him.

Incidentally, since I have told you elsewhere that courtship is a time of maximum deceit on the part of both parties, watch how they treat other people, especially their parents. For once they have you; that is how they will eventually treat you. Speaking of watching them, Luke 16:10 gives great counsel when choosing a mate. "He that is faithful in that which is least is faithful also in much: and he that is unjust in the least is unjust also in much." In the magazine article I mentioned above they were not quite ready to commit themselves, but they were finding that the more honest a person was, the less likely they were to cheat on their spouses.

"A good man out of the good treasure of his heart bringeth forth that which is good, and an evil man out of the evil treasure of his heart bringeth forth that which is evil: for of the abundance of the heart his mouth speaketh" (Luke 6:45). These are wise words that will help you choose the company of a good man. Another good idea to help you avoid finding the wrong mate is to take a psychology class.

Do not read romance novels. I know from observations that they will put notions in your head that you will not think about your husband. I suspect that this is because of the fact that a man marries a woman like his mom, and a woman seeks a man like her dad. Since subconsciously you view husbands as providers and father figures, this may be why you will entertain these romantic thoughts about other men and never about your husband. James 1:15 tells us that lust leads to sin, which leads to the death of our souls.

Berkeley, California, psychotherapist Elayne Savage says familiarity is a big reason people may choose someone like Mom or Dad as a partner. "When you grow up familiar with a certain type of person, you're attracted to that same type of person because it feels comfortable, whether you like it or not," says Savage, author of *Breathing Room: Creating Space to Be a Couple.*

"That's what people mean when they meet a potential partner and say, 'It feels like I've known him my whole life.'"

Rape or near-rape fantasies are central to romance novels, one of the perennial best-selling categories in fiction. Romance novels are often called "porn for women." Porn is all about sexual fantasies. In porn for men, the fantasy is sexual abundance–eager women who can't get enough and have no interest in a relationship. In porn for women as depicted in romance novels, the fantasy is to be desired so much that the man loses all control. Gleaned from Psychology Today written by Michael Castleman M.A. posted Jan 14, 2010.

Currently, there are 7 billion people on the earth. We are in no danger of extinction and quite probably are in more threat of overpopulation. So, do not fall for any feminist deception that you must find the superior mate for any fantasy of propagation of the human race unless, of course, you are a little Hitler looking to make a superior race. Truthfully, this is saying that feminists are looking for their superiors.

Here are a few things to do that will help you in your journey through life as well as in your search for a mate. In other words, develop some interests in yourself so you will have more than just sex to attract a guy. The feminist sure know how to brainwash you into thinking that is all men want. Life, the more you put into it, the more you will get out of it. Galatians 6:7 says whatsoever a man soweth he shall also reap. Same goes for your marriage. "For even when we were with you, this we commanded you, that if any would not work, neither should he eat" (II Timothy 3: 10). No one ever gets ahead without working at it.

Increase your vocabulary. This is the single most effective way to raise your intelligence. Studies show that vocabulary correlates more highly with intelligence than does any other individual factor measured on IQ tests[18]. Learning a foreign language will also increase your intelligence. Not all men prefer their women dumb. If they do, it could mean they may be intimidated by their wives. Do you really want to be married to a man like that?

Take music lessons. This will increase your cognitive level and broaden your horizons. Music affects your sense of creativity as well as providing a stronger sense of self-esteem. It will also give you some class. As a female today, you have access to the same public education available to everyone. Let no one deceive you into believing that you are handicapped due to your gender; this education is free. For some, it will be all that they will get; so, get all you can, while you can. Music lessons are available for free as well as language classes so, no excuses. I have met several women who were deceived by the feminists into believing they could not get an education because they were women. Believe me; this had a dramatic negative impact on their lives. The feminist truly will stoop to any level to make their lies seem to be the truth.

Dress well and behave appropriately as a lady should at all times. A real gentleman will be attracted to a classy lady. I once met a young lady who dressed like a lady and even acted like one. But she did not speak like one. Consequently, none of the boys her age treated her like one. Once she cleaned up her language though, they began to. If you are a lady and a guy does not respect you, shame on him. If you are not a lady, do not expect to be respected as one. In short, develop some interests in yourself so you have more than sex to interest a guy in you.

148

DRUGS

Yet another device of Satan's that parents need to concern themselves about. The boys will steal, and the girls will prostitute themselves to support any addictions they acquire. When it comes to drugs and sex, I wish I could get a dollar from every parent who has said, "not mine." Alcohol is considered a drug too; the only difference is that it is socially acceptable.

When I was twelve, I lived in Jacksonville Florida. One day, an old lady and her granddaughter came down the street in a cart pulled by a seedy old horse. You remember the kind with various junk hanging off of them. Ok, I am old but not that old, this was not an everyday thing. Well, anyways this old lady gave me a candy bar, a Hershey's almond joy. Yes, my memory is that good. I could go on but I won't. I showed it to my mother, and upon inspection, that candy bar had a little hole in the top. Needless to say, the next time that cart came around, there were words exchanged. That was a long time ago. The need to teach your children not to take anything from strangers and if they do to show it to you has only gotten worse.

My son was born with a birth defect, so I have spent a lot of time in the hospital with him, some of that in ICU. One of the other patients was an eight-year-old girl whose parents found her unconscious on the sidewalk in front of a store. This little girl almost died. It was two weeks before she could go home. I remember holding her and asking her how much she could remember before coming to the hospital. She could not remember anything prior to a week before she was found unconscious. It was sometime later before she could remember drinking some blue liquid from a small vile some man had given her. Why share this you ask? Today you must street smart your kids; their world is not as innocent as yours was. As I once explained to a child, it is not that every stranger is terrible; it is just that you do not know you can trust the person. Explain that there are some bad people out there and until you know you can trust them, don't. It is essential to educate children today but do not create such paranoia that causes them to live in fear. They may grow into adults with some problems.

I had an eighth-grade teacher who gave us some excellent advice that I remembered and followed. It was plain and simple: if you ever set a drink down in public, do not pick it up again. Years later, while in the Air Force, I set a drink down in the poolroom and walked away from it. On my return, I threw it into the trash. The guy standing next to me got mad and demanded to know why I had done that. A week later, an MP caught him putting something into someone else's drink.

Sadly, there is another drug called the date rape drug. A television documentary on the manufacturer of this drug demonstrated that there is no medicinal purpose for it at all. Despite this, the manufacturers refused to cease making it. They had made 100 million dollars that particular year off of it. Some companies are making lots of money on illegal devices so never doubt that they are out there. Despite being illegal even to possess this drug in the U.S., it is very likely quite prolific in many countries as well. The only thing the manufacturer agreed to do was put something in it that would turn a drink blue after 20 minutes. Whether they did it or not is another thing. Always be very careful about where you get your drinks. That is not just for the women; men have been known to be rolled for their wallets too.

GUYS ONLY

I have gotten a lot of feedback from people who asked me, "What about the guys?" Well, here it is. Even though this book is most likely to be read by the fairer sex, there is considerable information here for the men as well. To keep from repeating much of this material, I suggest you read it all. If you read between the lines, hopefully, you will learn how to spot and avoid a flawed woman. As I've said before, God is not one-sided, and both sexes can benefit from this material.

This material is about helping a girl to grow into a lady, among other things. That would be easier if there were more gentlemen in the world as well. One sex effects and influences the other despite any claims to the contrary. One thing men can do to help is refuse to accept a woman who is less than a lady. Another is to treat those who are true ladies with respect so more females will want to become ladies.

In my college health class one day, one of the female students brought in her younger sister. It came up that she was still a virgin, and she started to cry because there were no gentlemen who appreciated her for that. This is a great shame to those who call themselves men. It is time to accept the responsibility of the state of things today and to start living right. Recognize the great gifts women like this young woman are. Unfortunately, it is because of men's doings that there are not more like her out there to choose from. It is their responsibility to say no and yours not to ask.

Ephesians 5:22 commands women to submit unto their husbands. This does not mean she is inferior to you. As Proverbs

12:4 says, a virtuous woman is a crown to her husband. Her glory is your glory; encourage her to excel in all things. A good wife will not intimidate a man who is truly confident in himself. God commands husbands to love their wives as their own bodies. He that loveth his wife loveth himself (Ephesians 5:28.) A virtuous woman is indeed your better half. Is that what is being said when a man gets down on his knees to propose?

Therefore take heed to your spirit, and let none deal treacherously against the wife of his youth (Malachi 2:15B).

On a Christian radio station, the pastor was telling of a man who had committed adultery (dealt treacherously against his wife) and was tearfully requesting his wife's forgiveness. She said she could forgive him but could never trust him again.

Satan took the form of the serpent when he brought down man, God's perfect creation. If you seduce a virtuous woman, you are a snake in the grass. You have brought down another of God's creations just like Satan, and spoiled another man's favor from God. God really meant for a woman to be a gift to her husband. See how far you bring down a virgin if you seduce her!

Know ye not that ye are the temple of God, and that the Spirit of God dwelleth in you. If any man defile the temple of God him shall God destroy; for the temple of God is holy, which temple ye are (I Corinthians 3:16, 17).

This verse means to keep from destroying your temple with fornication; more importantly, do not defile a woman's temple. Never become a servant of Satan. A true gentleman would never leave a woman worse off than he found her. To enrich someone else's life is a pure act of love. For true gentlemen are as rare as a virtuous woman. Always strive for a higher value for yourself.

Read the quotation from the book *A Return to Modesty* by Wendy Shalit (P 50) again and make a note of the effect on a young girl who lacks her father's approval. Raising children is not just a woman's job. A father's presence and involvement in their lives is essential and continues to have an influence in their adult lives. If you do not think so, just watch the effect your mistakes will have on their lives. Learn from other people's mistakes, and you hopefully will not make the same ones.

I had a friend who told me how unhappy he was with the job his father had done raising him. I then asked him if he was not doing the same thing with his son. He replied that he did not know how to do a good job either. I told him that was a lie because he knew what he missed and wanted; those were the same things his son wanted.

Make it a priority to spend quality time with your daughter, just the two of you. There are many activities you can do together. Go bowling. Go fly a kite together – better yet, make one. Ice cream at a local parlor together has got to be a winner with any little girl. Do not be surprised if a grown daughter likes this too. If you have more than one child, have your spouse take the other(s) out to create more quality time. Next time, swap kids.

Teach your sons that women are not just for sex, and that "scoring" will not make a man out of them. Remember that sooner or later a young man will come around for your daughter's attention and affection. Perhaps, you should teach your son to treat a young lady as you hope this young man will treat your daughter. All young men should be taught from an early age to respect women. Then there will be more gentlemen in the world and fewer sexual assaults. No one should have to accept the responsibility but you if you are not a gentleman.

After all, why should a lady accept anything less than a gentleman? Also, tell your son that when he is on a date, he is likely holding someone else's wife and that someone out there is holding his. Consider the tale of David and Bathsheba in II Samuel chapters 11 and 12. King David sees Bathsheba bathing and lusts for her. Rather than being contented by one of his wives, he sends for her and lies with her. She conceives a child. When his attempt to hide it fails, he has her husband Uriah killed in battle. In Chapter 12:11, God sends Nathan to David to tell him that his wives will be given to his neighbors because he defiled another man's wife. Learn that even though a maid is not yet married, she is still meant to be. If you defile her, you deserve to have your wife defiled as well – just like David.

As stated earlier, all of this material applies to men as well as women, save that the husband is the head of the house. For more ladies to exist, there have to be more gentlemen who will not accept less than a real lady. Likewise, to make more gentlemen, women must not accept anything less. Both genders are responsible for the state of things today. The only way to make changes is to go against the flow and not be afraid to live right. For good lasting relationships are not based on sex after all.

If a female plays games with you, consider it her way of asking how much she can get away with. Run hard. Remember I have typed up a feminist speech and know this is the truth. Playing games are taught by the feminists and are a good indicator of whom you are involved with. Women have been misled to believe they will find out how committed men are to them by playing these games. I also told the females that the guys who put up with games only want to jump and dump them. If a female is older and still playing games, it's a good sign she has been jumped and dumped a lot. It's not a good idea to get involved with her, especially if she has not figured out that those games do not work.

I was discussing this once, and a woman made a comment about how mature people handled games. I replied, "Mature people do not play games." I attended a speech by a woman at my college who stated that there are 50-year-old girls and 20-year-old women. Marriage is tough enough but be certain it will be a lot tougher being married to a girl and not a woman.

"Give not thy strength unto women, nor thy ways to that which destroyeth kings" (Proverbs 31:3). I always wondered why I hated the games females played so much, now I know. They truly want to take away our strength as men. Remember Delilah how she perplexed Samson, pressed him daily with her words, and urged him so that his soul was vexed unto death (Judges 16:16). Tears and wiles are also signs of a bad woman. This is a result of Adam's failure to take control in the garden.

I cannot resist the urge to throw in I Corinthians 13:11: "When I was a child I spake as a child, I understood as a child, I thought as a child, but when I became a man I put away childish things." Needless to say, if as an adult you behave like a child, it will bring misery into your life. When you let childish things into your life, you invite misery. Put away all "childish things," especially the grown females who play childish games. Women do not play games, girls do.

As I have told the women elsewhere not to get involved with alcoholics, I have to tell you by far be certain that any involvement with a feminist will bring misery into your life. Even one of their own warns never to marry a feminist. Read this entire book to find out why! Do not bring home certain women's magazines. They are riddled with feminist teachings. For example, they tell women to have sex with their husbands only when they want, never when their husbands do. To a worldly feminist, sex is a tool and a weapon. The independence that the feminists teach is "me" oriented, not "we" and is for their gratification. Go ahead and get involved with one and it will be the one thing that will bring the most misery into your life.

I Corinthians 7:28 warns that those who marry will have trouble in the flesh. A feminist wife will cause even more troubles. I have heard too many men tell about how their wives love to crank them up. Be certain that worldly feminism is Satan's device; letting him into your life is undoubtedly going to ruin it and you.

Read the chapter about preventing sexual assault. Do not even call yourself a man if you rape someone. The next time you see a pretty woman you do not know but would like to, remember someone has been there before you and ruined her trust of strangers. Not enough gentlemen are in the world today for that beautiful stranger to trust you. Read the entire chapter. It should convince you rape is not about sex. And if you do think it is just sex and commit the crime of rape, you just may reserve your permanent place in hell.

"A good name is rather to be chosen than great riches, and loving favor rather than silver and gold" (Proverbs 22:1). Loving favor means to be well loved and to have the affections and esteem of all. A good name does not mean your surname. We cannot make many choices in what we get. Rather, a good name means to desire and seek out respect. One way to do this is, to be honest, and proper in our dealings with others. A real gentleman will treat a lady properly, and he will be known for it.

We all deal with insurance at one time or another in our lives. We take out home insurance, medical as well as car insurance. Take out some marriage insurance. There is one company, Lloyds of London that will insure just about anything. No, do not go to them for this marriage insurance. They would not insure anything with that much risk. Realize that this marriage insurance is going to cost you just like any other insurance, but it will pay you back.

- Keep the romance in your marriage.
- Set aside money in your budget for a date, at least, once a month with your wife.
- Flowers once in a while will go a long way too.

The first few chapters of Proverbs tell us of the virtues of wisdom and how it will make our lives prosper. "When wisdom entereth into thine heart and knowledge is pleasant unto thy soul. Discretion shall preserve thee; understanding shall keep thee" (Proverbs 2: 10-11).

Wisdom will deliver thee from the strange woman, even from the stranger, which flattereth with her words: "Which forsaketh the guide of her youth, and forgetteth the covenant of

157

her God" (Proverbs 2:17). To go into a strange woman is folly and will only bring death. "For her house inclineth unto death, and her path unto the dead. None that go unto her return again, neither take they hold of the paths of life" (Proverbs 2:18-19). This woman is certainly a servant of Satan. Adultery puts mankind on a path that leads to death. Notice in verse 17 where she forgets the covenant of God. The "guide of her youth" is her husband whom she is forsaking. The covenant that she ignores is her wedding vows.

Wisdom is valuable. It will protect you from the evil man and the seductive words of the adulterous woman. Proverbs 2:20-22 explains that those who pursue wisdom will have the knowledge required to avoid the wrong kind of people and have companions of good morals. The pursuit of wisdom will require work on man's part. God's truths are still valid even if man figures them out on their own. They are still true no matter how people twist the Word of God for their own purpose and agenda. I still recommend taking a physiology class whether in high school or college. It will help you in your journey when selecting a spouse.

Exodus 34:28 shows that the Ten Commandments are a covenant with God. Fortunately, God is a rock, never changing, and we know He can never break His covenant with man. Unfortunately, mankind is not a rock and is ever breaking his covenant. If not for the grace and mercy of God, none could inherit His kingdom; "For we all have sinned and come short of the glory of God" (Romans 3:23). This does not mean we can continue in sin. Let no one fool you about the importance of any of God's covenants with man, especially concerning marriage.

I Corinthians 6:13–20 discusses the folly of joining oneself to a harlot. Our bodies are the temples of God. Verse 16 shows us all that we are joined as one flesh with anyone we have sex with. An emotional union is also formed that will reach out beyond the physical union in your life. Many people of both genders who fall to temptation will base their relationships on this emotion. When it wears off, they will go looking for it in another person, leaving them unable to form a lasting, deep, meaningful relationship. Verse 18 says to flee fornication "Every sin that a man doeth is without the body; but he that committeth fornication sinneth against his own body." This should come as no surprise, for there are presently over twenty-seven STDs that can be contracted, thirty percent of which are incurable. This is in addition to the emotional baggage that fornication will bring. Everything you do will stay in your head for years.

Sex is more important to a smart woman. This is the type of woman to seek out; she is less likely to cheat on her husband. A woman will give you a better marriage than a girl. A woman who sleeps with strangers is no lady. Joining your temple of the Holy Ghost to a child of the Devil is tantamount to sleeping with the Devil. If you break your covenant with God, you may be thrown into the bottomless pit along with Satan. As long as we live, God's mercy is there for us if we will but reach out for it.

A foolish woman is clamorous: she is simple, and knoweth nothing. 14 For she sitteth at the door of her house, on a seat in the high places of the city, 15 To call passengers who go right on their ways: 16 Whoso is simple, let him turn in hither: and as for him that wanteth understanding, she saith to him, 17 Stolen waters are sweet, and bread eaten in secret is pleasant.

18 But he knoweth not that the dead are there; and that her guests are in the depths of hell (Proverbs 9:13-18).

Here again is proof that the smarter a woman is, the higher the value she places on sex. The foolish woman will sleep with strangers. And the men who turn in to her are just as simple. If this sounds like hellfire and brimstone, it just may be. Or is it the brutal truth? We are headed towards destruction if we continue to defile God's creation.

I happened to be in court one day when a man was getting divorced. He caught my attention because he was complaining about child support. It seems he was not left enough to support himself totally. So, I asked him why he was getting divorced. He had caught his wife cheating on him. I was curious as to how he met her in the first place. The funny thing was, he had met her in a bar and had sex with her the same night, but he could not figure out why she had cheated on him.

According to the proverbs of Solomon: "A wise son maketh a glad father: but a foolish son is the heaviness of his mother" (Proverbs 10:1). Do not break your mother's heart. Remember the previous reference to when a simple man will turn in unto the strange woman. A wise son heareth his father's instruction: but a scorner heareth not rebuke (Proverbs 13:1).

Do not pick a woman just because she is pretty but because you love her. For once the ravages of time work on her beauty, you will not be so happy if that was all that appealed to you and inspired you to marry her. You may not go to sleep physically as Rip Van Winkle did for 20 years, but someday, you will wake up to a different world. On the other hand, do not be afraid to ask a beautiful woman out. Too many have been heard to complain how lonely they are because men do not dare to ask them out; they think a beautiful woman is unobtainable.

My grandfather had a significant influence in my life, and he is about to influence yours. He once had a dog named Skipper; now, Skipper was a smart dog. Whenever he got into the car and went for a ride, he soon learned that it ended at the vets. So, it became difficult to get him into the car at all. He did love to go for a ride as most dogs do though, so what my grandfather did was take him for short trips starting about two weeks before his appointment at the vets. When the big day came, I can still remember Skipper running for the car when my grandfather called him. He never saw it coming. Not that you should treat women like dogs but if the only time you hug your wife is when you want sex, she knows what is coming. It is like being captured in a war. The first few seconds will determine if you are going to be really lucky and live.

"A good man obtaineth favor of the Lord: but a man of wicked devices will he condemn" (Proverbs 12:2). Again Proverbs 18:22 says, "Whoso findeth a wife findeth a good thing, and obtaineth favor of the Lord" I told the women if they want to catch the best husband, they will need some excellent bait. If you want a really good wife, you had better work on yourself also. Is it a valid expectation to ask a woman to preserve herself for an evil, foolish man?

Ask yourself, do you deserve an excellent godly woman? How do you do that? Let them know chivalry is not dead; plus, you must live a godly life. Give of yourself just like Jesus did. Be a gentleman and hold a door open; give up your coat. Most importantly, keep all promises or don't make them. Show kindness to all things, animals as well as people. Keep your conversations righteous. Possessions will not make you desirable to a real woman. Drive, determination, and commitment will go a long way.

A published study gave three reasons why a wife may cheat on her husband:

1) Lack of quality time
2) Inability to resolve a conflict
3) Lack of attention

I Corinthians 7 talks about not denying each other's sexual needs. Women are more emotional than men, and if you do not meet those needs as well, it will make them susceptible to the temptation to stray. Read this entire book to learn more about how females work.

If you ask a bunch of girls if they want to play tag, they will squeal with delight. Ask a group of boys, and they are just not interested. Why is this? It is in the females' psychological nature to love to be pursued all their lives. If you don't do it, they will look elsewhere. There is always someone willing to do it. Let your wife know you appreciate her; praise her continually. If you do, no other man will be able to fool her into thinking he can appreciate her more. A woman needs to feel loved; if not by you then she may look elsewhere. This requires physical contact as well as listening to her. Never put her down.

Rotate your best friend every two years or so. Most men who lose their wives will do so to their best friends. Always beware of the false teachers mentioned in II Timothy 3:6. Marriage is the single thing that you will work the most at in your entire life. If you don't want to work at it, then plan to fail. Does this give you any insight as to why so many marriages fail today? "Likewise, ye husbands, dwell with them according to knowledge, giving honor unto the wife, as unto the weaker vessel, and as being heirs together of the grace of life; that your prayers be not hindered" (1Peter 3:7).

I've told the women, so guys, you should know as well. Courtship is a time of maximum deceit on both parties' parts. What do deceivers use? Lies. Beware of liars. More likely than not when someone tells you they would not change a thing about you, they are lying. Make sure you discuss when and how many children you want before marriage. All women have a biological clock. This came from a woman, not me. All women want to appear pristine so doubling the number of sexual partners they have had is closer to the truth. Money is another topic to make sure you discuss.

You will never completely understand women. My son once asked me what makes the girls different when he was young. I told him I did not know, but if he ever figured it out, he could become rich. He asked me how, and I told him if someone could tell me I would pay then a hundred dollars and so would a lot of other men. I still remember one little girl's father laughing when he told him why he was asking his daughter so many questions.

HOMOSEXUALITY

The Lord is not slack concerning his promise, as some men count slackness; but is longsuffering to us-ward, not willing that any should perish, but that all should come to repentance (II Peter 3:9).

Since God is not willing that any should perish, this scripture states that God did not make anyone to perish by making them homosexual. Homosexuality is a choice! Note the word "effeminate" means homosexual.

Know ye not that the unrighteous shall not inherit the kingdom of God? Be not deceived: neither fornicators, nor idolaters, nor adulterers, nor effeminate, nor abusers of themselves with mankind, nor thieves, nor covetous, nor drunkards, nor revilers, nor extortioners, shall inherit the kingdom of God (I Corinthians 6:9-10).

At a health class I was taking, we had to discuss homosexuality. Yes, they have forced their way into our colleges and public schools, but prayer has been removed. During one of these discussions, studies were brought up that 80% of the population had homosexual thoughts. The statement that this made 80% of the population bi-sexual is inaccurate, to say the least. What Satan tempts us with does not make us anything. He also tempted Jesus. How we respond and deal with this temptation will determine who we are. James 1:13 tells us that God does not tempt man, which means only Satan tempts us. Recognize that Satan and not God puts thoughts of homosexuality into our heads. The excuse, "I cannot help myself" is a lie, because, in fact, it's a matter of a person simply giving into temptation. Since we are all tempted by Satan, there is nothing wrong with you if you have had those thoughts. Merely dismiss them for what they are, nothing more than temptation. Satan will leave you.

Have no fear, Psalms 27:1 says: "The LORD is my light and my salvation; whom shall I fear? The LORD is the strength of my life; of whom shall I be afraid?" Have no fear of Satan for God can protect us from him just as He forbade Satan to touch Job's life (Job 2:6).

Wherefore God also gave them up to uncleanness through the lust of their own hearts, to dishonor their own bodies between themselves: Who changed the truth of God into a lie, and worshipped and served the creature more than the Creator, who is blessed forever, Amen For this cause God gave them up unto vile affections: for even their women did change the natural use into that which is against nature: And likewise also the men, leaving the natural use of the woman, burned in their lust one toward another; men with men working that which is unseemly, and receiving in themselves that recompense of their error which was meet. And even as they did not like to retain God in their knowledge, God gave them over to a reprobate mind, to do those things which are not convenient; Being filled with all unrighteousness, fornication, wickedness, covetousness, maliciousness; full of envy, murder, debate, deceit, malignity; whisperers, Backbiters, haters of God, despiteful, proud, boasters, inventors of evil things, disobedient to parents, Without understanding, covenant breakers, without natural affection, implacable, unmerciful: Who knowing the judgment of

God, that they which commit such things are worthy of death, not only do the same, but have pleasure in them that do them (Romans 1:24-32).

In verse 24, we see further proof that God made no one to be homosexual in reference to the lust of his or her own heart. "Giving them up," means that He has written them off as lost souls and that they are without restraint in their lusts. An excellent example of this lack of self-control is found in Genesis Chapter 19. In the story of Lot, we are at the point where all the men of Sodom surround Lot's house and want to have sex with the angels that are within. In Genesis 19:11, the angels smite the men outside with blindness. The lust of sodomy was so great in them that they wearied themselves looking for the door in their blindness, rather than freaking out that they were all suddenly blinded. Romans 1:25 tells us those who practice and advocate homosexuality have turned the truth of God into a lie.

A coroner who wrote a book about his career stated that whenever a body that was severely beaten was discovered, he knew they were looking for a homosexual. Our government conducted a program called the Manchurian candidate where they tried to program people to be killers. After many trials, it was abandoned because it is impossible to program someone to murder. Homosexuals are indeed under no restraint and have no compunctions when it comes to serving their own pleasures. If there were more godly people in the world, there would be less violent crimes committed because of people being given over to their reprobate minds.

As have been proven above, I reiterate: Homosexuality is a choice and the statement "I cannot help myself" is a blatant lie. Now that you have God's truth let no one fool you.

In Romans 1:26, we see that the women change their natural use into an unnatural use. This means that they turned into lesbians. In verse 27 of the same chapter, the men abandon the natural use of women and turn to men. That means homosexuals. Combine I Corinthians 7 with these scriptures and know that anyone who propagates the line "It is not natural for a man to love a woman" is turning God's truth into lies.

Undeniably, any group that fights for lesbian rights, as the feminists do, has got a lesbian among them somewhere. For more than 30 years, the feminist movement has been a "Leader in the struggle for lesbian rights" with same-sex marriage being "a center stage issue." Their subtle influence on all of their followers is evident in their instructions to play cruel games with men. It should now be apparent why they propagate the lie that "It's not natural for a man to love a woman." When and if you ever hear this from a feminist/lesbian ask her if she thinks all those marriages survive on just sex. When they have destroyed women's relations with men, they will be ready to embrace those whom they have disillusioned towards men openly. Hopefully, this helps convict both sexes that involvement with feminists invites ruin.

Where will this put you in God's kingdom if you join the worldly feminists? What normal woman would want anything to do with them? "Whosoever, therefore, resisteth the power, resisteth the ordinance of God: and they that resist shall receive to themselves damnation" (Romans 13:2). "For it is written, As I live, saith the Lord, every knee shall bow to me, and every tongue shall confess to God" (Romans 14:11). Yes, indeed, and someday, all lying shall cease. Until then, we must learn to discern the truth.

Satan is the father of all lies, and there is no truth in him (John 8:44). Do not be confused or deceived. Witnessing to people is not the same as associating with them. Associating with homosexuals will expose your soul to their lies and give them the opportunity to work on you. "Be not deceived: evil communications corrupt good manners" (I Corinthians 15:33). Never expose your children to them and do not let them into your home as God instructs in Deuteronomy 7:26. I know of two separate women who did, and when they evicted them from their homes, the homosexuals were angry; they let their true intentions be known. They were trying to turn their children to homosexuality.

They do not have an organization called Queer Nation for nothing. Never let them into your home via television either. That is not wholesome family entertainment. The way television is going today; they should have a new rating for homosexual content. It seems to be creeping into every program.

Neither shalt thou bring an abomination into thine house, lest thou be a cursed thing like it: but thou shalt utterly detest it, and thou shalt utterly abhor it; for it is a cursed thing (Deuteronomy 7: 26).

Let's not forget those who choose to wear the clothing of the opposite gender. It's a real shame for the children of today to see those who do. This fits right into the shock and awe that they wish to impose upon the rest of us.

The woman shall not wear that which pertaineth unto a man, neither shall a man put on a woman's garment: for all that do so are abomination unto the LORD thy God (Deuteronomy 22:5).

"He that justifieth the wicked; and he that condemneth the just, even they both are an abomination to the LORD" (Proverbs 17:15). Never give a lesbian or homosexual a sign of approval by saying even one of them is "all right" or join any group that openly embraces them. It flies in the face of God every time a Christian says, "So and so was all right."

Never forget there is none like God the next time you think about saying those words (II Samuel 7:22). Matthew 12:36 warns us, "Every idle word that men shall speak, they shall give account thereof in the day of judgment."

More than once, I have observed fathers who felt giving hugs and loving their sons would turn them into homosexuals. Nothing could be further from the truth. Little boys who lack father figures are the targets of the homosexuals. Make sure you are in their lives and not just present.

We shall see in the story of Asa that all men are not without a reasonable amount of time to turn to God from their sins. Notice that Asa became diseased in the 39th year of his reign and died in the 41st year. The lesson here is that God is not an impatient God but will give us time to come to him before we die. If Asa had called upon the Lord between his 39th and 41st years, he could have been saved from this disease.

Were not the Ethiopians and the Lubims a huge host, with very many chariots and horsemen? yet, because thou didst rely on the LORD, he delivered them into thine hand. For the eyes of the LORD run to and fro throughout the whole earth, to show himself strong in the behalf of them whose heart is perfect toward him. Herein thou hast done foolishly: therefore from

henchforth thou shalt have wars. Then Asa was wroth with the seer, and put him in a prison house; for he was in a rage with him because of this thing. And Asa oppressed some of the people the same time. And, behold, the acts of Asa, first and last, lo, they are written in the book of the kings of Judah and Israel. And Asa in the thirty and ninth year of his reign was diseased in his feet, until his disease was exceeding great: yet in his disease he sought not to the LORD, but to the physicians. And Asa slept with his fathers, and died in the one and fortieth year of his reign (2 Chronicles 16:8- 13).

In verse 9, we see that God is ever seeking to show himself strong on behalf of those with good hearts. This is evident in verse 8 where God protected Asa from his enemies because he sought the Lord. Indeed, the Lord is our strength, of whom should we be afraid?

AIDS

Yes, indeed, "the wages of sin is death." Not everyone who sins will contract AIDS, and not everyone with AIDS has necessarily sinned. AIDS is more of reaping of what man has sown.

For the wages of sin is death; but the gift of God is eternal life through Jesus Christ our Lord (Romans 6:23).

The World Health Organization (WHO) reports that since the beginning of the HIV/AIDS epidemic, more than 70 million people have been infected with the HIV virus and about 35 million people have died of HIV. Globally, 36.9 million [31.8–43.9 million] people were living with HIV at the end of 2017. If not for the violence, those numbers would make war seem tame. After the discovery of penicillin in 1928 and prior to the appearance of AIDS, there was a short period where mankind was in no danger of death from a sexually transmitted disease (STD). God is patient and long-suffering, but we did not get the message to follow His ordinances, and we shall ever suffer the consequences. Find a cure for one STD, and another will come along to replace it as a killer.

Mankind has the means to eradicate every STD, but unfortunately, we will never use the means to do it. STDs have been around throughout history, as has this method. This is not some panacea or an amazing new discovery; it is quite old-fashioned, as some would call it. It is two simple words: abstinence and fidelity. That is it, pure and simple. The only problem is getting everyone, and I mean everyone, to practice these simple instructions. Regrettably, we are never going to be able to accomplish this because we will never get everyone to live by such principles. History has proven this time and time again. We cannot control the world around us to that extent, but we can make this a part of our own lives. Only then can you live free of any fear of a sexually transmitted disease.

Harping on safe sex has not worked. Now, the word abstinence is included in any material on AIDS or safe sex. "Without addressing behavior, the response to prevention strategies will always be limited. We will create some results here and there, but unless there is a fundamental change in behavior, there will be no drastic change in the evolution of the epidemic," said Elhadj As Sy, head of the UN AIDS program for East Africa.[19]

The people of the world have slowly come to be aware that they cannot have their cake and eat it too. Good luck getting the world to practice safe sex, for the only safe sex is the way God planned it for us. In case you have not read any other chapters yet, that means not before marriage or with anyone else but your spouse. Only then will you be immune to any of the consequences of premarital sex and adultery.

I took a class called Human Sexual Awareness to complete the requirements for the health section of my B. S. degree. This class consisted mainly of women and had a few men. Needless to say, the topic of safe sex came up, to which I asked the other students, would any one of them have sex with someone they knew had AIDS, if they were using a condom? Not surprisingly, not one person said he or she would. I could not resist the temptation to find out why. The bottom line was that they just did not trust the condom. Then I asked, given that, why they would have sex with a stranger. I stated that their partner might have it and not even know or just plain not care. No one replied; there was only silence. I suggest you ask yourself the same question and think long and hard.

In the gym at college one day, I ran into one of my classmates, and we got to talking. The topic of sex with strangers came up, and his attitude was that you "just wear a glove" as he put it. Glove, in this case, was slang for a condom. The disturbing thing that makes me remember this is that he also told me he used to be a junkie and all the friends that he shot up with now had AIDS except him. He called it a miracle. Well, let me tell you, I didn't believe it for a minute and you should not either.

Not two blocks from my home there used to be a billboard. Once it had a picture of a beautiful woman with boxing gloves and a "come hither look." This was an ad for condoms, and it stated that they were 98.8% effective. In other words, they will fail 12 out of a thousand uses. On the website of AIDS Information Switzerland, they state, "If a sexual partner is infected with HIV, the risk of transmission can be reduced but not excluded, by the use of condoms."

Have you ever seen the AIDS virus? It is so hard to cure by the way because it is just that, a virus. Like the common cold virus, we cannot kill them without killing the host. Not desirable at all, especially if you happen to be the host. The AIDS virus looks like a sphere with spikes sticking out from it. The real deadly part comes in when you take into consideration its size, which is just 50 nanometers a lot smaller than one of our cells. That is about one-sixteenth the size of our cells. Now consider inside a woman with no skin layer and no condom or one of those twelve that will fail. It would not take very much pressure with its spikes and small size for just one of those viruses to penetrate her cells. Is safe sex beginning to sound more like a one-lifetime partner to you?

I maintain that you do not know anyone well enough even to consider having sex with them until you know you can safely give them a loaded gun. By the way, you never really know anyone until you marry him or her. So, do not even think of sex before marriage!

PREVENTING SEXUAL ASSAULT

I hope you have figured out that this material is about how to become a lady. That might make you wonder what the subject of sexual assault has to do with remaining a lady. The sad facts are that there are rapists out there, lying in wait. The primary purpose for including this subject is to discuss how a lady would deal with this situation should it become necessary. Regretfully, it is required far more often than most realize. A prison guard once told me that half of all prisoners were in jail for rape.

One in five girls will be sexually assaulted in the U.S., almost 50 percent of sexual assaults happen before people reach 18 and the vast majority of victims are girls. The perpetrators are boys and men they know (82 percent of attacks are perpetrated by non-strangers). One of the worst aspects of the rape culture is that it's impossible for girls and women to know who is and isn't actually a rapist.

These numbers are repeatedly verified and, although boys are also raped, the fact of rape functions to affect the lives of all of the girls and women you know. Yes, there is a risk of false rape accusations, but while most people think 50 percent of rape allegations are false, comprehensive reviews show the rate to be between 2-8 percent, similar to the number for other crimes.

It is an underreported crime;[20] at best guess there is a forcible rape every two minutes in America.[21] A newspaper article in the early '80s calculated that by the year 2000, one out of every three women would have been raped at least once.

Unfortunately, gang rape has also been on the rise. I clipped a news article from a paper in 1985, which said between 1973 and 1982 an estimated 1.5 million women and an estimated 123,000 males were victims of rape.

Most psychologists agree that rape is not for sexual desire but the result of anger or the need to assert power. The majority of rapists are young men who have sexual outlets available to them. They either are married or are dating women they have sex with voluntarily.

When anger against women is the motive, the perpetrators are violent and the act unpremeditated with the intent to degrade their victims. Beware of drug users as some of them induce great fits of rage as does alcohol in some people. I remember reading an article about a man who dragged a woman behind a building at a party and shot her in the head. One of the times my son was in the hospital; a three-year-old boy was admitted whose mother had beaten over forty percent of his body in a drug-induced rage. I can still remember his crying. Before he left, he was displaying violence against the nurses. Anger against women cannot be justified, but I am sure this played out throughout his life. Hitler's hatred of the Jews was traced back to one woman.

Rapes done out of the need to assert power are pre-planned, and the victim is stalked. This type of rapist may be compensating for feelings of helplessness. They also display a need to control people in other ways as well. Never date the schoolyard bully. He likes to control people, and that is what rape is about; the ultimate control over someone else. Psychologists can attest to the fact that this desire to control spills over into other aspects of rapist's lives. Avoid arrogant people. To see a pretty woman and just take her if that is not arrogant what is?

With the rise in the number of homosexuals, it is no longer a problem for women only. This means that no matter who you are, there is a chance it could happen to you. It would be a good idea to discuss this subject with your spouse or potential mate since a lot of marriages do not survive rape. I will give you a hint, guys: it does not help to accuse women of "asking for it" to protect your male egos. It would help for you to tell them that you love them and that no man can ever steal that away from them.

> If a damsel that is a virgin be betrothed unto an husband and a man find her in the city and lie with her, then ye shall bring them both out unto the gate of that city. And ye shall stone them with stones that they die; the damsel, because she cried not, being in the city; and the man, because he hath humbled his neighbor's wife: so thou shalt put away evil from among you. But if a man find a betrothed damsel in the field, and the man force her, and lie with her: then the man only that lay with her shall die: But unto the damsel thou shalt do nothing; there is in the damsel no sin worthy of death: for as when a man riseth against his neighbor, and slayeth him even so is this matter: For he found her in the field, and the betrothed damsel cried, and there was none to save her (Deuteronomy 22: 23-27).

The first thing to examine here is the fact that we are dealing with a betrothed virgin. Notice that no mention is made of the non-virgin. If the damsel is in the city and does not cry out, she is to die also. This is in contrast to being in the field where there was no one to save her. The damsel in the city is not innocent as the damsel in the field, and she is to be dealt with as an adulteress. This says loud and clear that if a woman cries rape, it goes without saying that God commands someone to rescue her. If all you can do is call the police, you should do so to save her. Definitely, do not stand around and without helping or idolize the rapist as some sort of a hero.

Remember that a Christian man or woman will not require or expect anything in return for helping others. Likewise, Proverbs 17:13 says, "Whoso rewardeth evil for good, evil shall not depart from his house." If someone does help you, at least, say thank you.

The following is just my opinion and is being offered simply as food for thought. Not fully understanding the Trinity, I believe that God does not know of the death of the flesh like mankind will. I wonder if here God is referring to the death of the spirit, the second death. Any way that you look at it, I would not want to be in either the rapist or the victim's shoes to find out. This is not to condemn anyone but to encourage people not to break this law. God's mercy is infinite if we but ask for it. Sorry for repeating myself but we must ask for forgiveness in order to receive it. As a final thought let's examine Matthew 12:31 "Wherefore I say unto you, all manner of sin and blasphemy shall be forgiven unto men: but the blasphemy against the Holy Ghost shall not be forgiven unto men." God's mercy is limitless and amazing.

While you consider my opinion, it is also believed that if the victim does not report the rape after it has happened, it is the same as not crying out for help during the rape. Since this scripture refers to a betrothed damsel, it applies equally to a married woman "because he hath humbled his neighbor's wife."

Consider two couples for a moment: One woman who, having her conscience seared as with a hot iron, commits adultery and hides it from her husband; the other woman is raped, but also hides it from her husband and faces him every day as if nothing happened. There is no difference between the two, for the husband's marriage bed has been defiled. In both cases, the woman hides it from her husband. The bottom line here is that a real lady could not face her husband every day and hide something like rape from him. This should be discussed before marriage by all couples.

Rape is not a crime of passion but one of violence. It is the ultimate control over another person, so never date the schoolyard bully. I am not going to delve into the different types of force used, but if you think being beaten is passionate, you should seek psychological counseling. Only a rapist can become sexually aroused by violence.

Although some people may tell you that being raped is simply like having sex with someone whom you did not want to, this assertion is wrong. As stated before, it is not just sex. If it were, then perhaps, they should legalize rape. After all, if it is just sex, so what if they have to hold you down? Some people accuse me of making too much of it. If God deems rapists worthy of death, there is no such thing as making too much of it. It can and does render some women insane. It does not sound like a small thing when one rape victim counseling a new victim told her, "There will come a time when you will forget for a whole day." Victims can and do suffer post-traumatic stress syndrome. After you have been raped, there will never be a day in the rest of your life where you have not been violated.

Initially, a victim is in shock and often will ask in disbelief "Why me?" After the initial fear and anxiety, other symptoms will manifest themselves. They may lose their appetites, develop headaches (resulting from the silent rage rape is often called) insomnia and fatigue. Some will be plagued by nightmares and irrational fears for years afterward. Some will become unable to maintain a job as well as maintain a normal sex life. These symptoms may persist for years afterward.

This is one instance where an ounce of prevention is worth more than a pound of cure. Rape can and does happen anywhere, anytime. I know of a case where a bank teller was raped at her bank during business hours. And no one stopped it.

It is certainly not my desire to educate the public on ways to commit this heinous crime. I also recommend that you look carefully at any and all advice you are given to avoid rape. Yes, even mine, for I am hardly an expert either. James 4:17 compels me to provide you with the best advice I can, though. Incidentally, a woman juror is 35% harder to convince of rape than a man is.

There are many statistics about rape. The ones I am about to share are gleaned from my memory of what has been disseminated through the media.

- 40% of all rapes started out as simple burglaries.
- A burglar commits three-fifths of all rapes in the home.
- 40% of all rapes happen in the daytime.
- 80% of the victims know who their attackers are.
- The average rapist has 25-30 victims.

- Most likely to be attacked are single women between the ages of 15-25.
- Pornography encourages rape by depersonalizing women.

Here is some advice on how to prevent rape; once again, I am no expert, so examine my advice carefully:

- Never hitchhike or pick up a hitchhiker. Remember that I said it is not just a woman's problem any longer. Never live alone if you can help it.
- Do not publish your phone number; it will also list your address. Do not think using your first initial will fool anyone.
- Do not leave your car windows down when you park anywhere. Buy a car with air conditioning. Remotes do work in the summer also. Always lock the doors to your home and car.
- Do not ever tell a stranger where you live. If you are being followed, do not lead the person to your home.
- Do not ever leave anything with your address on it in a public place (like trash cans). This applies to females of all ages.
- Do not ever tell anyone you could never go through a rape trial. Not even another woman; for I know of women who have helped their husbands commit rape. It is rare, but it can and does happen. They are called opportunists rapists. They will rape only when they think they can get away with it; meaning that they will strike when they know their victim does not care or would never report it.
- If you use an answering machine, get a male friend to record your message.

- Carry mace and make sure it has not expired. Always know where you are.
- Own a cell phone and always carry it with you
- Cell phones today have GPS devices in them so if you are being stalked, turn it off. However, the police can also use it to find you if you need help. If you absolutely do not need to be there do not, especially at night. Rapes typically take place between 6 p.m. and midnight.
- Neither men or women should ever use or participate in pornography of any kind. It turns women into pieces of celluloid with no feelings or emotions.
- Never have sex voluntarily with strangers. This will only serve to put credence to the myth that it is just sex and will do nothing to reinforce the respect men should have for women.
- If you want men to have a higher level of respect for women, do not propagate the myth that it is just sex.
- Make it harder to rape you than somebody else by following the above advice and then search for more. This may sound cruel, yes, but the truth is rapists are out there.

If you are ever raped, do not be ashamed of it. It happens to a lot of women, and if it happens to you, you are not alone. If you are raped, go to a hospital emergency room even if you are absolutely sure you could never prosecute. Doing so does not require you to press charges. You could contract a sexually transmitted disease and or AIDS. They have an AZT cocktail to help you if your attacker does have AIDS. Yes, I know someone who was attacked by an individual with AIDS. While I was in New Jersey, there were a couple of articles in the paper about just that type of attack. Also, if you change your mind about pressing criminal charges later, it will be that much easier for you if you have gone to the hospital right away. Those tadpoles have DNA.

Don't be ashamed if you have an orgasm during the rape. As explained to a little girl whose father had raped her, if someone hits you it hurts because that is the way God made your body to work. Sex is the same way. It is just the way God made your body to function. Yes, it is horrible to be forced to have sex, but it does not mean you helped your attacker or asked for it.

As one rape victim said, it is no fun to be raped. Realize that at first, you will not fully understand the consequences as to what has happened to you. It is called the silent rage for a reason. This means that later it will have a much more negative influence in your life. It is not going to go away easily. Victims can and do suffer post-traumatic stress syndrome.

It is up to women to unite and prove that rape will not be tolerated. It will not get any better until you send a message that you will no longer suffer quietly. In other words, more victims have to let people know that they have raped the wrong women. Many women have asked how this could happen to them. Perhaps, that is because society as a whole believes it only happens to women who deserve it. Realize that no one deserves to be raped, and everyone needs to stop viewing the victim as dirty. That includes other women as well.

Only then will more women find the courage to come forward. The more women who do come forward, the more rapists will go to jail, and the safer the world will be for all.

The bottom line is anyone who makes the victim sorry is helping the rapist. Even the victim is assisting the rapist if she does not come forward. Surprised? Remember that the average rapist has 25 victims, and if you do not report him, you are helping him to hurt someone else. I know this will hurt a lot of women; for this will be foremost on their minds. It is best to confront your demons right off. They will only get bigger later on. Undoubtedly some women do not report rape because of their lack of confidence in the legal system. You can't complain and say they failed you if you do not give the law a chance.

It seems that a lot of the victims coming forward in the #MeToo movement may not have reported the assault right when it happened. Two things we should learn from this is that 1 it will bother you for a long time afterwards. 2 If you want credibility later you should not wait to report it.

Incidentally, if you feel you are being persecuted or denied justice, call the F. B. I. Obstructing the law or harboring a fugitive from justice is illegal for everyone, and the F. B. I. has a particular division just for handling corrupt law enforcement officers, even judges. You will find them listed in the front of your phone book or call information. They have offices in Boston, Massachusetts and Roanoke, Virginia to name just a few. Go online to *www.fbi.gov* also to obtain local phone numbers.

Report a potential trafficking situation. If you suspect that a child in your city may be a victim, call the 24-hour National Human Trafficking Resource Center hotline at 888-373-7888, or submit your anonymous tip online at *polarisproject.org*. "Child trafficking is hard to spot," says Sarah Jakiel, deputy director of the Polaris Project, the nonprofit that runs the hotline. "The biggest red flags are children who are working when they should be in school, have an unreasonable lack of freedom, and show any signs of physical abuse." Since the hotline opened in

2007, they've helped more than 5,000 victims find safe housing, counseling, and legal help in states including Florida and Texas. "Children are lured here from places like Guatemala, El Salvador, and Mexico with the promise of education," says Kathleen Morris, who leads the *International Rescue Committee's anti-trafficking programs* in Seattle. "They know they'll have to work a little bit, but they often never get to go to school and are forced into jobs with long hours and no pay. What many people don't realize is that this is happening in places we see on a regular basis, like small coffee shops and construction sites we drive by. It's hidden in plain sight."

When I published my other book How to Prevent Sexual Assault: How to Detect and Defeat Todays Spy Technology I also put seven petitions on the then available Whitehouse.gov site.

One was to make mandatory sentencing when a jury convicts a rapist. Another was to put Chemical Castration on the law books. Then another to make castration mandatory when the victim was 14 or younger.

They don't make it easy, you need 150 signatures before your petition appear on the web site for the public to view. I still cannot believe I could not find the required 100 thousand women's signature for chemical castration.

I wish I had the attentions of the politicians as the feminist do. If you are one of the feminist's leaders, I challenge you to take up this cause and do some real good for women. I can think of nothing better than to make our country safer for women.

THE WORLDLY FEMINISTS

The feminists view children as traps for women. I hate to admit it, but they are right in a sense when a teenager gets pregnant her chances of getting married decline. Not many young men want an instant family. Finishing even high school will become difficult. However, the problem is that they consider teenagers women. Your chances of going to college are not good either and living on welfare is not a bright future.

Little wonder then that feminists fight so hard for teenagers to get abortions without their parents' consent or knowledge. In some states, minors can get abortions without parental consent or knowledge. Is yours one of them? No doubt about it the correct way to uplift women is to teach them that sex can and does lead to pregnancy and to encourage abstinence as the only 100 percent means to avoid ruining your life. Maybe it would go a long way to point out that at a young age girls are just sex objects to the boys. That means they have no other interest in them since they are not of age to marry.

I was sitting in a class one-night listening to a public radio station. The program was titled "Are women citizens?" They would sing a little fast song then come on with some statements about conditions thousands of years ago for women. I could not help wondering what effect that had on the women of today other than to stir them up to follow the people on the program's rhetoric/cause. The statement that stands out in my memory was how those women in biblical times who came before the king/judges were killed.

They quoted Esther from the Bible and stated that she was killed for seeking justice. Now anyone who knows his or her Bible knows this is a blatant lie. Sadly, there are a lot of uneducated women who no doubt believe this. I cannot help but wonder given the number of women whom I have heard say that they were Christians and feminists, why they would follow such liars. The female making the program would ask, "Are women citizens? I don't think any politicians today would dare say we are not" as if anyone was trying to.

I receive the Smithsonian magazine, and one month (March 2012), a magician (Teller of Penn & Teller) was divulging some of his trade's secrets. One was that it's hard to think critically if you're laughing. "We often follow a secret move immediately with a joke. A viewer has only so much attention to give, and if he's laughing, his mind is too busy with the joke to backtrack rationally." He would make them laugh with a joke, at the time when he would move his hands right in front of the audience to perform his trick, and no one noticed. It works the same way when the feminists do the fast song trick or give a speech real fast. You are so focused on keeping up and taking it all in that you are not thinking. At the same time, they put their lies in your brain, and you are not even aware of it.

I took a test once to work for the census bureau, and two women were testing with me. It became apparent that they were not well educated and were cheating on the test. When the person running the test came in, we all got into a conversation about it, and they stated they were told/taught that females were never to ask questions in school. I told them that I had never heard or seen that in any school I attended including college and that they had been lied to. Naturally, I wanted to know who told them that.

It came as no surprise to me that it was the feminists. I told them that it was a lie to hold them back and make the feminists lies appear to be true.

For rebellion is the sin of witchcraft, and stubbornness is as iniquity and idolatry (I Samuel 15:23).

Witchcraft is a manipulation to get someone to do what you want them to. Little wonder the feminists embraced and propagated Diana Wicca. Their complete agenda is a seduction to influence others for Satan. One of their seductive tricks is to sing a song really fast as mentioned above, then make a statement and go right back to the fast song. That's their way of planting their false statements in your mind without any contest from you.

How appropriate for the feminists to have embraced Wicca; they are to blame for some of its creation. This is from *Webster's Online Dictionary:* "In particular Diana Wicca is a religion whose origins lie within radical feminism." Still, want to call yourself a Christian and a feminist? Understand that feminism is all about the rebellion of God's design in our creation.

The feminist movement is a pure rebellion of God's desires and ordinances for mankind. You don't think so? On April 30, 2016, Fox News published that Washington -The House Armed Services Committee approved an annual defense policy bill early Thursday morning that includes a provision that would require women to register with the Selective Service System. Do you still, want a select few radical women to speak for you? Look where it is leading you to. WAR. Nowhere in the Bible does God ever command a woman to go to battle. You are not physically or mentally made for it.

In the book, *The Female Brain* by Louann Brizendine M.D., it states that we all started out as females. At about eight weeks into a pregnancy, if the child is to be a male, a surge of testosterone kills off cells in the communication center and grow more in the sex and aggression centers. The female brain will grow more connections in the communication and emotions centers of the brain. Not to be sexist but the consequences are that females are not good at separating emotional from rational. Real men do not freak out over a mouse but most women will.

Imagine you, a female, in a war on the front lines. The person next to you takes a direct rocket hit. You look over, and there is nothing left but one smoking foot in his/her boot. A few seconds later, the person's head lands about 20 feet away. Graphic enough for you? Can you say Post Traumatic Stress Disorder? I guarantee more women will suffer from this than men. Even when the Israelite armies were wiping out the people in the Promised Land, God commanded them to rest afterward. Today, a tour of duty is limited to a set number of days to reduce the chances of PTSD happening.

Let the feminist keep on speaking for you; someday, women will, indeed, serve in combat mandatorily. There are and always will be distinct differences between men and women. We should work to get along not work for Satan's destruction of God's plans for us. Satan succeeds when we are fighting against each other.

What say I then? That the idol is anything, or that which is offered in sacrifice to idols is anything? 20 But I say, that the things which the Gentiles sacrifice, they sacrifice to devils, and not to God: and I would not that ye should have fellowship with devils. 21 Ye cannot drink the cup of the Lord, and the cup of devils: ye

cannot be partakers of the Lord's table, and of the table of devils (I Corinthians 10:19-21).

How can a woman call herself a feminist and a Christian? Call yourself a feminist and ask yourself, will God call you one of His? When the scripture says ye cannot be partakers of the Lord's table and the table of the Devil it means that God will deny you. "Do we provoke the Lord to jealousy?" (1Corinthians 10:22). Are we stronger than He?

The so-called socialist feminists believe that the government should provide childcare facilities. So, they can have it all – a career and a family. It is self-evident that it is not possible to have a career and a family without some support network. The only ones who will come out short in this arrangement are the children. Not to make any anti-government statements but what caring, loving mother would want to leave her child in their care?

The feminist hailed the pill as liberation on the sexual front. They held up promiscuous men as the ideal they wanted to achieve and have casual sex also. No wonder they view marriage as oppressive because it limits their ability to have sex whenever and with whomever they desire. After marriage, sex becomes a tool that will be rationed out in response to performance if and when they desire.

They tell their followers that playing games will show you how committed a man is to you. Trust me; I know; as I said before, I have typed up one of their speeches. They really teach women to play games so they can learn how much men will do to get sex. They often fail to realize that after men have had the horizontal party, they are done with them. This is the feminists' desire so you will become disgusted with men and turn towards their sexual orientation. Same-gendered.

One fallacy I want to disprove that the feminists propagate is that it is a sign of weakness if a man thanks you for sex. How much more subservient can you be than to let a man use you for sex with no regard or appreciation for you? Here, we are talking about their use of sex, not God's design for it. You will have to use sex to become the man chaser the feminists want to turn you into. Let's think about this from a different perspective; do some thinking for yourself for a change. Time was when it used to be called "Getting lucky." Now, it sounds more like he will be lucky if he does not get a disease.

I know I am repeating myself but the feminists are targeting young girls and teaching them this sexual liberation. They fight for free contraceptives for children and abortions without parental consent or knowledge. I fear many young girls fail to recognize when a guy is only interested in sex. They fail to work at a relationship because they don't have to. As long as they are having sex, the boys will come around. Take this attitude into a marriage, and it is no wonder so many fail.

The single scripture that the feminists attack the Promise Keepers for is, "Wives submit unto your husbands." They seem to have a real hard time following God's ordinances. It appears that they know more than God and choose to defy Him by deeming that marriage makes a woman subservient to her husband.

Some of the information I have shared with you has come directly from the feminists' website. Others have come from my interactions with feminists and some from my direct observation of women's magazines. I was married once and unavoidably had them in my home.

But evil men and seducers shall wax worse and worse, deceiving, and being deceived. But continue thou in the things which thou hast learned and hast been assured of, knowing of whom thou hast learned them (II Timothy 3:13-14).

Have you ever tried to contact your congressman? It's not as easy as it sounds. The feminists have no problems though. I spoke to a man named Mike (Dad's against Divorce) who sat outside the governor's office for six weeks on a hunger strike to get to speak with him. The closest he ever got was when the governor would come up to him and say, "Hi Mike." Yet, Mike would watch the feminist come and go as they pleased into the coveted office.

Why mention this? Because some congressmen cave into feminist pressure whether the populace wants it or not. It is evident by the sneaky, underhanded way we now have same-sex marriage in Massachusetts. One of the reasons given was that they had more important things to consider. In other words, they knew the homosexuals would keep coming back, so they caved and denied the public the right to decide what kind of world they and their children will live in. That's right; Massachusetts' citizens never got to vote on same-sex marriage. Anyone who says different is lying.

TEN LIES OF FEMINISM

Article contributed by Probe Ministries Visit Probe's website Feminism made promises it couldn't keep. Probe's Sue Bohlin examines ten lines of feminism identified by Dr. Toni Grant from a Christian perspective.

This essay examines the ten lies of feminism that Dr. Toni Grant suggests in her book *Being a Woman*[22].

At its inception, the feminist movement, accompanied by the sexual revolution, made a series of enticing, exciting promises to women. These promises sounded good, so good that many women deserted their men and their children or rejected the entire notion of marriage and family, in pursuit of "themselves" and a career. These pursuits, which emphasized self-sufficiency and individualism, were supposed to enhance a woman's quality of life and improve her options, as well as her relations with men. Now, women have had to face the fact that, in many ways, feminism and liberation made promises that could not be delivered[23].

Lie #1: Women Can Have It All

The first lie is that women can have it all. We were fed an illusion that women, being the superior sex, have an inexhaustible supply of physical and emotional energy that enable us to juggle a career, family, friendships and volunteer service. Proponents of feminism declared that not only *can* women do what men do, but we *ought* to do what men do. Since men can't do what women can do–have babies–this puts a double burden on women. It wasn't enough that women were already exhausted from the never-ending tasks of child-rearing and homemaking; we were told that women needed to be in the workforce as well, contributing to the family financially.

Scripture presents a different picture for men and women. The Bible appears to make a distinction between each gender's primary energies. The commands to women are generally in the realm of our relationships, which is consistent with the way God made women to be primarily relational, being naturally sensitive to others and usually valuing people above things. Scripture never forbids women to be gainfully employed; in fact, the virtuous woman of Proverbs 31 is engaged in several part-time business ventures, in real estate and manufacturing. Nonetheless, it is the excellent care of her husband, her children, her home and her community that inspires the praise she is due. Titus 2 instructs older women to mentor younger women, and teach them to care for their husbands and children and homemaking responsibilities. The God-given strengths of a woman were given to bring glory to God through her womanly differences

Lie #2: Men and Women are Fundamentally the Same

Apart from some minor biological differences, feminism strongly suggested that males and females are fundamentally the same. Culture, it announced, was responsible for turning human blank slates into truck-wielding boys and doll-toting girls. This lie has been very effective at changing the culture. Men, for instance, tend to be more goal-oriented and competitive, where women are more relational and cooperative. Men are active; women are verbal. This is intuitively obvious, but it is often new news to high school and college students.

They have been so immersed in this cultural myth that they had accepted it without question. The truth is that God created significant differences between males and females. We can see evidence of this in the fact that Scripture gives different commands for husbands and wives, which are rooted in the differing needs and divinely-appointed roles of men and women.

Lie #3: Desirability is Enhanced by Achievement

The third lie of feminism is that the more a woman achieves, the more attractive and desirable she becomes to men. The importance of achievement to a man's sense of self–an element of masculinity that is, we believe, God-given–was projected onto women.

Feminism declared that achieving something, making a mark in the world, was the only measure of success that merited the respect of others. Women who believed this myth found themselves competing with men. Now, competition is appropriate in the business and professional world, but it's disastrous in relationships.

Men do respect and admire accomplished women, just as they do men, but personal relationships operate under a different set of standards. Men most appreciate a woman's unique feminine attributes: love, sensitivity, her abilities to relate. Women have been shocked to discover that their hard-won accomplishments haven't resulted in great relationships with men. Sometimes, being overeducated hampers a woman's ability to relate to men. Men's egos are notoriously fragile, and they are by nature competitive. It's threatening to many men when a woman achieves more, or accomplishes more or knows more than they do. Feminism didn't warn women of the double standard in relationships: that achievement can and does reap benefits in our careers, but be a stumbling block in our relationships.

The question naturally arises, then, Is it wrong for a woman to have a higher degree of education than the man in a relationship? Is it troublesome when a woman is smarter than the man? Should a woman "dumb down" in order to get or keep her man? In the words of the apostle Paul, "May it never be!" A woman living up to the potential of her God-given gifts brings glory to God; it would be an insult to our gracious God to pretend those gifts aren't there. The answer is for women to understand that many men feel threatened and insecure about this area of potential competition, and maintain an attitude of humility and sensitivity about one's strengths; as Romans exhorts us, "Honor[ing] one another above yourselves" (12:10)

Not surprisingly, God already knew about the disparity between the sexes on the issue of achievement. Throughout the Bible, men are called to trust God as they achieve whatever God has called them to do. It's important for men to experience personal significance by making a mark on the world. But God calls women to trust Him in a different area: in our relationships. A woman's value is usually not in providing history-changing leadership and making great, bold moves, but in loving and supporting those around us, changing the world by touching hearts. Once in a while, a woman does make her mark on a national or global scale: consider the biblical judge Deborah, Golda Meir, Margaret Thatcher, and Indira Ghandi. But women like these are the exception, not the rule. And we don't have to feel guilty for not being "exceptional."

Lie #4: The Myth of One's "Unrealized Potential"

Lie number four says that all of us–but especially women–have tremendous potential that simply must be realized. To feminism's way of thinking, just being average isn't acceptable: you must be *great*.

This causes two problems. First, women are deceived into thinking they are one of the elite, the few, the special. The reality, though, is that most women are ordinary, one of the many. All of us are uniquely gifted by God, but few women are given visible, high- profile leadership roles, which tend to be the only ones that feminism deems valuable. We run into trouble when we're operating under a set of beliefs that don't coincide with reality!

Consequently, many women are operating under unrealistically high expectations of themselves. When life doesn't deliver on their hopes, whether they are making class valedictorian, beauty pageant winner, company president, or neurosurgeon, women are set up for major disappointment. Just being a cog in the wheel of your own small world isn't enough.

This brings us to the second problem. A lot of women beat themselves up for not accomplishing greatness. Instead of investing their life's energies in doing well those things they *can* do, they grieve what and who they are *not*. Just being good, or being good at what they do, isn't enough if they're not the *best*. Romans 12:3 tells us, "Do not think of yourself more highly than you ought." Rather than worrying about our unrealized potential for some sort of nebulous greatness, we ought to be concerned about being faithful and obedient in the things God has given us to do, trusting Him for the ultimate results. And we ought to not worry about being ordinary as if there were some stigma to it. Scripture says that God is pleased to use ordinary people because that's how He gets the most glory. (See 1 Corinthians 1:26-31.) There is honor in being an ordinary person in the hand of an extraordinary God.

Lie #5: Sexual Sameness

The fifth lie of feminism is that men and women are the same sexually. This lie comes to us courtesy of the same evil source that brought us the lies of the sexual revolution. The truth is that women can't separate sex from love as easily as men can. For women, sex needs to be an expression of love and commitment. Without these qualities, sex is demeaning, nothing more than hormones going crazy.

The cost of sex is far greater for women than for men. Sex outside of a committed, loving relationship–I'm talking about marriage here–often results in unplanned pregnancy, sexually transmitted diseases, and profound heartbreak. Every time a woman gives her body away to a man, she gives a part of her heart as well. Sexual "freedom" has brought new degrees of heartache to millions of women. The lie of sexual equality has produced widespread promiscuity and epidemic disease. No wonder so many women are struggling with self-esteem!

God's commands concerning sex take into account the fact that men and women are not the same sexually or any other way. He tells us to exercise self-control before marriage, saving all sexual expression for the constraints of a marriage relationship, and then to keep the marriage bed pure once we are married. When we follow these guidelines, we discover that God's laws provide protection for women: the security of a committed relationship, freedom from sexual health worries, and a stable environment for any children produced in the union. This high standard also protects men by providing a safe channel for their sexual energies. Both chaste single men and faithful husbands are kept safe from sexual diseases, unwanted pregnancies with women other than their wives, and the guilt of sexual sin.

Lie #6: The Denial of Maternity

Many women postponed marriage and childbearing to pursue their own personal development and career goals. This perspective denies the reality of a woman's reproductive system and the limitations of time. Childbearing is easier in a woman's 20s and 30s than in her 40s. Plus, there is a physical cost; science has borne out the liabilities that older women incur for themselves and their babies. Midlife women are more prone to have problems getting pregnant, staying pregnant, and then experiencing difficult deliveries. The risk of conceiving a child with Down's Syndrome is considerably higher in older mothers[24]. Fertility treatment doesn't work as well for women over 40[25].

There is also a spiritual dimension to denying maternity. When women refuse their God-ordained roles and responsibilities, they open themselves to spiritual deception and temptations. 1 Timothy 2:15 is an intriguing verse: "But women will be saved through childbearing." One compelling translation for this verse is, "Women will be *kept safe* through childbearing," where Paul uses the word for *childbearing* as a sort of shorthand for the woman's involvement in the domestic sphere–having her "focus on the family," so to speak[26]. When a married woman's priorities are marriage, family and the home, she is kept safe–protected–from the consequences of delaying motherhood and the temptations that beleaguer a woman trying to fill a man's role. For example, I know one married woman who chose to pursue a full-time career in the commercial real estate, to the detriment of her family. She confessed that she found herself constantly battling the temptation to lust on two fronts: sexual lust for the men in her office and her clients, and lust for the recognition and material things that marked success in that field. Another friend chose her career over having any children at all and discovered that like the men in her field, she could not separate her sense of self from her job, and it ultimately cost her her marriage and her life as she knew it. The problem isn't having a career: the problem is when a woman gets her priorities out of balance.

Lie #7: To Be Feminine Is To Be Weak

In the attempt to blur gender distinctions, feminists declared war on the concept of gender-related characteristics. These qualities that marked women feminine softness, sweetness, kindness, the ability to relate well–were judged as silly, stupid and weak. Only what characterized men–characteristics like firmness, aggressiveness, and competitiveness–were deemed valuable.

But when women try to take on male qualities, the end result is a distortion that is neither feminine nor masculine. A woman is perceived as shrill, not spirited. What is expected and acceptable aggression in a man is perceived as unwelcome brashness in a woman. When women try to be tough, it is often taken as unpleasantness.

Unfortunately, there really is a strong stereotype about "what women should be like" that merits being torn down. A lot of men are threatened by strong women with opinions and agendas of their own, and treat them with undeserved disrespect. But it is not true that traditionally masculine characteristics are the only ones that count.

There really is a double standard operating, because the characteristics that constitute masculinity and femininity are separate and different, and they are not interchangeable. To be feminine is a special kind of strength. It's a different, appealing kind of power that allows a woman to influence her world in a way quite distinct from the way a man influences the world. It pleased the Lord to create woman to complement man, not to compete with him or be a more rounded copy of him. 1 Corinthians 11:7 says that man is the image and glory of God, but the woman is the glory of man. Femininity isn't weakness; it's the glorious, splendid crown of humanity.

Lie #8: Doing is Better Than Being

In his book *Men Are From Mars, Women Are From Venus*[27], John Gray pointed out that men get their sense of self from achievement, and women get their sense of self from relationships. Feminism declared that the male orientation of *what you do* was the only one that mattered; *who you are*, and how important you are to the people in your world, didn't count for as much.

This lie said that active is good, passive is bad. Traditional feminine behaviors of being passive and receptive were denounced as demeaning to women and ineffective in the world. Only being the initiator counted, not being the responder. "To listen, to be there, to receive the other with an open heart and mind–this has always been one of the most vital roles of woman. Most women do this quite naturally, but many have come to feel uneasy in this role. Instead, they work frantically on assertiveness, aggression, personal expression, and power, madly suppressing their feminine instincts of love and relatedness."

Women's roles in the family, the church, and the world are a combination of being a responder and an initiator. As a responder, a wife honors her husband through loving submission, and a woman serves the church through the exercise of her spiritual gifts. As an initiator and leader, a woman teaches her children and uses her abilities in the world, such as the woman of Proverbs 3. God's plan is for us to live a balanced life--sometimes active, sometimes passive; sometimes the initiator, sometimes the responder; at all times, submitting both who we are and what we do to the Lordship of Christ.

Lie #9: The Myth of Self-Sufficiency

The ninth lie is the myth of self-sufficiency. Remember the famous feminist slogan that appeared on everything from bumper stickers to t-shirts to notepads? "A woman without a man is like a fish without a bicycle." The message was clear: women don't need men, who are inferior anyway. The world would be a better place if women ran it: no wars, no greed, no power plays, just glorious cooperation, and peace.

The next step after "women don't need men" was logical: women don't need anybody. We can take care of ourselves. Helen Reddy's hit song "I Am Woman" became feminism's theme song, with the memorable chorus, "If I have to, I can do anything / I am strong / I am invincible / I am woman!"

Of course, if women don't need anybody except themselves, they certainly don't need God. Particularly a masculine, patriarchal God who makes rules they don't like and insists that He alone is God. But the need to worship is deeply ingrained in us, so feminist thought gave rise to goddess worship. The goddess was just a female image to focus on; in actuality, goddess worship is worship of oneself[28]. *I once saw a woman who had tattooed "Goddess" on her forearm. I was not impressed. As in who are you trying to fool?*

The lie of self-sufficiency is the same lie that Satan has been deceiving us with since the Garden of Eden: What do you need God for? We grieve the Lord's heart when we believe this lie. Jeremiah 2"13 says, "My people have committed two sins: they have forsaken Me, the spring of living water, and have dug their own cisterns, broken cisterns that cannot hold water." God made us for Himself; believing the lie of self-sufficiency isn't only futile, it's a slap in God's face.

Lie #10: Women Would Enjoy the Feminization of Men

The tenth lie of feminism is that women would enjoy the feminization of men. Feminists believed that the only way to achieve equality of the sexes was to do away with role distinctions. Then they decided that that wasn't enough: society had to do away with gender distinctions, or at the very least blur the lines. Women embraced more masculine values, and men were encouraged to embrace more feminine characteristics. That was supposed to fix the problem. It didn't. *Read Appendix D for more on this topic.*

As men tried to be "good guys" and accommodate feminists' demands, the culture saw a new type of man emerge: sensitive, nurturing, warmly compassionate, yielding. The only problem was that this "soft man" wasn't what women wanted. Women pushed men to be like women, and when they complied, nobody respected them. Women, it turns out, want to be the soft ones–and we want men to be strong and firm and courageous; we want a manly man. When men start taking on feminine characteristics, they're just wimpy and un-masculine, not pleasing themselves or the women who demanded the change. There is a good reason that books and movies with strong, masculine heroes continue to appeal to such a large audience. Both men and women respond to men who fulfill God's design for male leadership, protection, and strength.

Underlying the women's liberation movement is an angry, un-submissive attitude that is fueled by the lies of deception. It's good to know what the lies are, but it's also important to understand what God's word says so that we can combat the lies with the power of His truth.

APPENDIX A

A True Tale of Two Sisters.

This is a true story of two sisters beginning when the oldest was twelve. Her oldest daughter is now twelve. To this day, neither is a Christian. I met this family through a group that we were all in. It starts out with an offhand remark I made about sex. Regrettably, I had assumed this kid knew what I was talking about. However, since I had opened the bag and let the cat out, I proceeded to bell the cat.

It was a bit difficult considering she was not a Christian and had no understanding of God's virtues. As best as I could, I explained why she should wait for her husband. I focused on giving her a sense of self-worth and told her the reasons for not having sex before marriage. For example, she would know if the boys were interested in her for who she was as opposed to just for sex. I remember pointing out that if she did have sex, all her classmates would know because her partner would very likely tell everyone. Her husband would not want to hear about her previous sex partners on their wedding night either.

This 12-year-old was hanging around with some 28-year-olds who were not ladies at all. She decided to stay away from them after realizing that they were not good examples.

She had heeded my advice to be careful about how she turned someone down for a date. She thanked me in her high school years because one of her boyfriend's told her he had witnessed her turn someone else down. It inspired him to want to get to know her.

She had been inspired by some terrible advice because of her association with bad company and running away from home. As a result, this girl was headed for a hard life. However, after she gained a new understanding of the value of her body and made changes in her life, she went on to become quite a young lady.

Now, her younger sister is a different story. I never had the chance to have the same conversation with her. The height of my influence came one day when I was visiting, and the older sister was about 16. I asked her how her younger sister was doing. She told me she was running away and not listening to her mother. She asked me to talk to her sister just as I had done with her. I suggested she might listen to her more than any of us adults. So off she went upstairs to talk to her sister. The only thing I can say changed in her little sister was the plan she had made to meet a boy in the woods behind the house later, which she did not do, especially when her mother found out.

Flash forward to when the oldest sister was about 20. I called to see how she was doing. Naturally, she was quite annoyed with me when I asked her if she was still a lady, which she was. After explaining that I simply wanted to know how well and long our conversation had influenced her, she understood. Then she expressed her anger at me because there were no gentlemen who appreciated her for her virtue. Incidentally, the last time I saw her she was absolutely beautiful. I asked her if she was not shooting herself in the foot because she did not seem to appreciate a man who valued her for that.

Then I proceeded to ask her if she knew anyone who was having sex that had gotten married. I pointed out to her that her sister who had moved out right after graduation and was then an unwed mother was not having any luck either.

After mentioning one more woman who made the same mistake, I told her that those women who were having premarital sex were not having any better luck than she was at getting married. I told her to stop shooting herself in the foot and chasing off suitors by mocking their respect for her. She is now presently married with two girls, and her younger sister is now divorced.

APPENDIX B

Samson and Delilah

The tale of Samson begins in Judges 13 and ends in chapter 16.

Chapter 13 opens with the Israelites under bondage to the Philistines for doing evil. An angel of the Lord appears unto Manoah's wife. He tells her that she shall have a child despite being barren and that no razor is to touch the child's head. The angel tells her he is to be a Nazarite, and he shall begin to deliver Israel from the Philistines. This chapter ends with the child's birth, and he was called Samson.

Chapter 14 – Samson sees a Philistine woman and tells his parents to get her for his wife. His parents know not that this is from the Lord and try unsuccessfully to talk him out of it. As they are with her parents, a young lion attacks Samson, and he kills it with his bare hands. After a while, Samson returns to take his wife. Turning aside Samson sees the lion's carcass with bees and honey in it. He takes some and shares it with his parents. Samson made a feast as was the custom and they brought thirty companions. Samson gives them a riddle, and if they solve it, he will give them thirty sheets and thirty changes of clothes. If they cannot solve it, he gets the same from them.

The riddle was this: Out of the eater came forth meat, and out of the strong came forth sweetness. They could not solve it, so they threatened to burn his wife and her father's house if she did not get the answer from him. She cried before Samson until he relented the last day. The men said unto him "What is sweeter than honey? And what is stronger than a lion."

So, Samson went into town and killed thirty men for their garments and gave it to those who answered the riddle. This made him angry, and he returned to his father's house, but his wife was given to whom he used as a friend. Chapter 15 – In the harvest, Samson sets out to visit his wife. Only to find out she had been given away to another. Samson went and caught three hundred foxes. He set their tails on fire and let them go in the cornfields and vineyards. When the Philistines learn who had done this, they burnt his wife and her father to death. So, Samson takes revenge and slaughters many. The Israelites bind Samson and give him to the Philistines. The spirit of the Lord came mightily upon him, and he slew a thousand of them with the fresh jawbone of an ass.

Chapter 16 is where Samson meets Delilah and falls in love with her. The lords of the Philistines offer her eleven hundred pieces of silver each to find the way to defeat his great strength. She tries three times unsuccessfully to find out. Each time Samson gives her a false method, which she tries on him as he sleeps on her lap. When she presses him daily with words so that his soul is vexed unto death, he tells her all. This time as he sleeps, she has his head shaved and binds him. When she cries, "The Philistines be upon thee, Samson," he is taken prisoner and blinded. They make him perform women's work and grind in prison.

His hair eventually grows again. About this time, the Philistines have a feast to their God, and as their hearts become merry, they call for Samson that he might make sport for them. They set him between the pillars of their temple. Samson prays to God to give him back his strength this last time. He pushes on the pillars with all his might, and the house falls down. In death, Samson killed more Philistines than he did in his life.

APPENDIX C

The Full Armor of God

The full armor of God consists of:

<u>A belt to go around the waist</u>

"Stand, therefore, having your loins girt about with truth" (Ephesians 6:14a). Telling us to stand means we are not to attack the Devil for God is to defeat him. The Lord is our strength and protector; we are not to be afraid to stand against Satan (Psalm 27:1).

<u>Breastplate</u>

"And having on the breastplate of righteousness" (Ephesians 6:14b). This is the righteousness of Christ that will protect our hearts just as it protects the soldier wearing it.

<u>Shield</u>

"Above all take the shield of faith." With it, we shall be able to quench *all* the fiery darts of the wicked (Ephesians 6:16).

<u>Helmet</u>

Represents the helmet of salvation (Ephesians 6:17a).

<u>Sword</u>

"The sword of the spirit, which is the word of God" (Ephesians 6:17b).

In Ephesians 6:10, Paul instructs us to be strong in the Lord. The power of His might will strengthen us so we can do all things through Christ (Philippians 4:13). Verse 11 instructs us to use the whole armor of God. Anything less will weaken your ability to withstand Satan's wiles. Our battle is not a physical one like the foot soldiers but a spiritual one against the powers of darkness (vs. 12). In verse 15, our feet are to be shod with the preparation of the gospel. Here, we are told to keep our paths towards God because, in the Bible, our feet are symbolic of our ways. Giving us a clear conscience and peace that we may stand boldly in the evil day.

Since all churches are only turning out its maidens to be 14% purer than non-churched girls, someone has failed.[1] Either the church and parents have failed to give their daughters the full armor, or the girls have chosen not to wear it all. To guide our young and lost, we must show them the path of righteousness with love and understanding. This material is intended to illuminate the way by showing them they can resist and, most importantly, by inspiring them to want to endure. Giving them a sense of the higher value of self and the love God has for them is the desired objective of this material. The tale of two sisters is a good example that this has worked for a non-Christian. Make no mistake; it can work for the church as well.

APPENDIX D

It is simply amazing how such a tiny minority in our country, just three-tenths of a percent has forced a national debate about whether the public bathroom they visit should or should not match the gender of their plumbing.

As CNS News reports, *Dr. Paul R. McHugh, the Distinguished Service Professor of Psychiatry at Johns Hopkins University and former psychiatrist-in-chief for Johns Hopkins Hospital, who has studied transgendered people for 40 years, said it is a scientific fact that "transgendered men do not become women, nor do transgendered women become men. All such people, he explained in an article for The Witherspoon Institute, "become feminized men or masculinized women, counterfeits or impersonators of the sex with which they 'identify.'"*

Dr. McHugh, who was psychiatrist-in-chief at Johns Hopkins Hospital for 26 years, the medical institute that had initially pioneered sex-change surgery – and later ceased the practice – stressed that the cultural meme, or idea that "one's sex is fluid and a matter of choice" is extremely damaging, especially to young people.

Dr. McHugh says those who wish to change their gender suffer from a psychiatric condition, not an accident of birth. *Gender dysphoria—the official psychiatric term for feeling oneself to be of the opposite sex—belongs in the family of similarly disordered assumptions about the body, such as anorexia nervosa and body dysmorphic disorder," said McHugh. "Its treatment should not be directed at the body as with surgery and hormones any more than one treats obesity-fearing anorexic patients with liposuction," he said.*

Perhaps, the most tragic part of this new trend is the consequence. After the immense pain and hardship of transitioning, a high percentage of transgendered individuals eventually take their own lives.

When "the tumult and shouting dies," McHugh continued, "it proves not easy nor wise to live in a counterfeit sexual garb. The most thorough follow-up of sex-reassigned people—extending over 30 years and conducted in Sweden, where the culture is strongly supportive of the transgendered—documents their lifelong mental unrest." "Ten to 15 years after surgical reassignment, the suicide rate of those who had undergone sex-reassignment surgery rose to 20 times that of comparable peers," said McHugh.

GLOSSARY

Agape
1. Nonsexual love that is wholly selfless and spiritual.

2. Christian love. Selfless love felt by Christians for their fellow human beings.

Admonish
1. To rebuke someone mildly but earnestly.

2. To advise somebody to do or, more often not to do something

Apostasy
The renunciation of a religious belief of allegiance.

Befall
To come to pass; happen

Chastity
1. The state or quality of being chaste or pure.

2. Celibacy; Virginity

Chastity Belt
Any of various devices supposed to have been worn by medieval women and maidens to prevent sexual intercourse.

Christian
Christ-like.

Churlish
1. Crass characteristic of somebody who's ill breed.

2. Unkind and grumpy surly, sullen or miserly

Cognitive
1. Concerned with the acquisition of knowledge by use of reasoning, intuition or perception.

Covenant	Solemn agreement that is binding on all parties.
Gracious	1. Characterized by kindness and warm courtesy.
	2. Merciful compassion.
Helpmate	A helpful companion or partner, especially a spouse
Help meet	A helpmate, especially a wife.
Loins	The part of a human being on each side of the spinal column between the hipbone and the false ribs
Love	(agape) Seeking the highest good for another.
Mammon	Material wealth or possessions especially as having a debasing influence.
Nazarite	A Jew of biblical times consecrated to God by a vow to avoid drinking wine, cutting the hair, and being defiled by the presence of a corpse.
Secular	denoting attitudes, activities, or other things that have no religious or spiritual basis.
Virtue	1. The quality of moral excellence, righteousness, and responsibility; and probity; goodness.
	2. Conformity to standard morality or mores, as by abstention from vices; rectitude.
Virtuous	1. Exhibiting virtue; righteous: virtuous conduct.

2. Possessing or characterized by chastity; pure: a virtuous woman

Wile   1. A deceitful stratagem or trick.

2. A disarming or seductive manner, device, or procedure.

3. Trickery; cunning; deceit.

Wiles   To influence or lead by means of wiles; entice, lure.

REFERENCES

1. *Why Wait?* by Josh McDowell and Dick Day Here's Life Publishers, San Bernardino, CA (1987, p. 24)

2. Caption from the bottom of a story in *Readers Digest*.

3. H. H. Rowley, "The Interpretation of the Song of Songs," in The Servant of the Lord. P197

4. See Parsons, p 402. "Notes on Song of Solomon" Found http://soniclight.com/constable/notes/pdf/song.pdf

5. June 03, 1994 By Los Angeles Times

6. *The Complete Metalsmith* by Tim McCreight Davis Publications, Worcester MA (1982, p. 114).

7. *A Return to Modesty* by Wendy Shalit Touchstone Books; (January 2000)

8. *Hollywood Fashion Machine* (June 10, 2000). Documentary about Max Factor.

9. Gleaned from the front cover of a women's magazine.

10. Late Schuyler Butler, then senior pastor at Belmont St. Baptist Church Worcester MA.

11. *Why Love is not Enough* by Sol Gordon, Ph.D. Bob Adams, Holbrook MA. (1988, p. 17).

12. Quoted by a doctor at a local HMO.

13. Quoted from TV ministry Real Life with Gerald Mann, Austin TX.

14. American Psychological Association March issue of Journal of Personality and Social Psychology

15. John Mark Ministries
http://jmm.aaa.net.au/articles/4903.htm

16. http://www.hec.ohio-state.edu/famlife/divorce/demo.htm

17. Furstenberg, Jr., F. F., Nord, C. W., Peterson, J. L., & Zill, N. The life course of children of divorce: Marital disruption and parental contact. AMERICAN SOCIOLOGICAL REVIEW, 48, 656-668.

18. *Mensa Think-Smart Book* by Dr. Abbie F. Salny and Lewis Burke Frumkes
Harper and Row, New York (1999, p. 9).

19. AIDS and the African (Front page article) *Boston Sunday Globe* Oct 10, 1999.

20. "Four of ten rapes go unreported." (article). *Worcester Telegram* 3/85, Worcester, MA.

21. From FBI statistics.

22. Toni Grant, *Being a Woman: Fulfilling Your Femininity and Finding Love.* New York: Random House, 1988.

23. Ibid, 3.

24. March of Dimes, "Pregnancy After 35,"
     www.marchofdimes.com/professionals/14332_1155.asp.

25. Jodi Panayotov, "IVF & Older Women - How Successful
     is IVF After 40?" ezinearticles.com

26. Andreas Kostenberger, "Saved Through Childbearing?"
     (*CBMW [The Council on Biblical Manhood and Womanhood]
     News*, Sept. 1997), p. 3.

27. John Gray, *Men Are From Mars, Women Are From Venus*.
     New York: HarperCollins, 1992.

28. Mary Kassian, *The Feminist Gospel* (Wheaton, Ill.:
     Crossway Books, 1992), p. 159.

REVIEWS

Darla Ortiz

Wow, what an amazing book! I was completely sucked in from the beginning, and am so impressed with Daniel Hanson's bravery in challenging the 'status quo' and what society keeps pushing on women in such a harmful way. This book is loaded with insightful arguments, and Mr. Hanson has the great ability to pull from Scripture the most applicable passages to really underscore his message. It is clear that he is quite learned in regards to religious and philosophical Study and that he cares about the spiritual wellness of women and girls and the health and sanctity of a family unit. It was very well-written and riveting, but not a 'fast' read-- it should be carefully and thoughtfully studied and talked about. So many great discussion points here, I must have highlighted over a dozen passages. Hope to read more from him in the future and recommend to readers of Christian and Spiritual lifestyles/Parenting.

Meg King

"God's Feminist Movement" by Daniel Hanson was actually far more interesting and deeply insightful than I initially expected it to be (no offense to the author). I just wasn't sure what I was getting myself in for, but as I started reading, I was transfixed by Mr. Hanson's knowledge of the Bible, scripture, philosophy, and of life in general, and the impact that certain ways of thinking or behavior can do serious harm to a woman, her family, and all of society... There is a lot of information here, research, Scripture and personal narrative, and the way he writes and puts it all together is very moving, eye-opening, and ultimately transformative. "God's Feminist Movement" is an absolute 'must read' for anyone wishing to raise children in God's vision for them. I feel like Mr. Hanson does a fantastic job of relating his perspectives and information in an easy to digest and very readable manner, and it will definitely open your eyes and change the way you think about what is accepted behaviors, versus what God desires of us. It does discuss sexuality in depth, so probably best suited for mature Christian readers.

Peter Myles

In this book, Hanson writes engagingly and fascinatingly, exploring the complexities that exist in our society. With a close focus on the family, a basic social unit; the author explores prudent ways that the society can use to face contemporary issues of moral decadence such as divorce, immorality, and how to relate with members of the opposite sex. The book is a recommended read for parents, educationists, teenagers and those who are courting or in marriage. Hanson explores one of the complex endeavors in human history; being a feminist and a Christian; he interestingly weaves contradicting issues in a precise manner. Indeed; this book is a must read for all, highly recommended!

NOTES

NOTES

CPSIA information can be obtained
at www.ICGtesting.com
Printed in the USA
JSHW030850220622
27296JS00001B/49